BECOMING A LIFE COACH

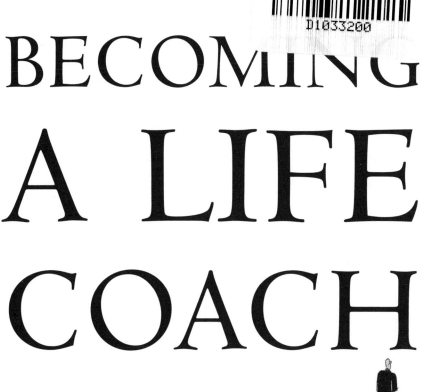

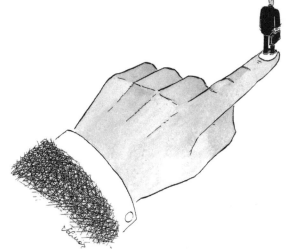

A COMPLETE WORKBOOK *for* THERAPISTS

DAVID SKIBBINS, PH.D., CPCC

New Harbinger Publications, Inc.

Publisher's Note

This publication is designed to provide accurate and authoritative information in regard to the subject matter covered. It is sold with the understanding that the publisher is not engaged in rendering psychological, financial, legal, or other professional services. If expert assistance or counseling is needed, the services of a competent professional should be sought.

Materials from the International Coaching Federation (ICF) used with permission.

Distributed in Canada by Raincoast Books

Cover design by Amy Shoup
Cover image by Spots Illustration/Jupiter Images
Text design by Michele Waters-Kermes
Acquired by Tesilya Hanauer
Edited by Amy Johnson

Library of Congress Cataloging-in-Publication Data

Skibbins, David, 1947-
    Becoming a life coach : a complete workbook for therapists / David Skibbins.
        p. cm.
    ISBN-13: 978-1-57224-500-6
    ISBN-10: 1-57224-500-X (Paperback)
    1. Personal coaching. 2. Psychotherapists. I. Title.
BF637.P36S55 2007
158'.3--dc22
                                        2007018500

09   08   07

10   9   8   7   6   5   4   3   2   1

First printing

This book is dedicated to Plato. Despite his aristocratic bias, he was the first to demonstrate the power of coactive coaching. In his dialogue *Meno*, he showed his students how a completely uneducated slave boy could be brought to understand the Pythagorean theorem—that era's equivalent to the modern theory of relativity. His questions accessed the natural intelligence and creativity inherent in all humans. For this, he is the great-great-grandfather of coaches everywhere.

CONTENTS

FOREWORD

When I was introduced to life coaching ten years ago, I had a thriving practice as a psychologist and business consultant. Coaching was a natural addition to my array of services, but at the time there was no manual available for therapists who wanted to become coaches. I had to figure it out as I went along. Now, thanks to David Skibbins, there is this delightfully informative manual to help therapists explore the possibilities. If you are considering adding life coaching to your professional services, *Becoming a Life Coach* is a worthwhile investment. Even if, as a therapist, you are simply curious about the profession of life coaching, you'll find this book useful.

For starters, David has succeeded in writing a book that clearly and thoroughly makes distinctions between coaching and therapy. He outlines the differences in assumptions, goals, and skills in very practical and straightforward language—and with a sense of humor, too! It's a breath of fresh air to have this clarity in writing. The matter-of-fact framework David provides forms the intellectual foundation every therapist needs to understand in order to succeed at life coaching.

In addition to teaching you about the profession of life coaching in general, this book will give you a good feel for the coaching process. David's concrete examples, case studies, and exercises illustrate what skills are necessary to be a successful coach and what skills you'll easily be able to transfer to coaching from therapy, as well as the obstacles therapists typically face when they become coaches. The most valuable information, though, comes from completing the exercises in each chapter, which will help you explore your skills, values, and strengths; set goals; and lay out action plans. You'll also be able to pinpoint areas that need work for you to become successful as a coach. In essence, the exercises let you try on coaching like you would a new outfit—without having to buy a whole new wardrobe. As an added bonus, you'll be able to use many of these same exercises with your coaching clients.

Finally, *Becoming a Life Coach* explains the ins and outs of developing and running a success-ful coaching business. David provides practical tools and sensible business advice that will help you discern whether or not life coaching is for you. He also includes a thoughtful, informative discussion of ethical guidelines for life coaching.

So get ready to find out if coaching is a good match for you personally and professionally. Roll up your sleeves, sharpen your pencils, get to work, and have fun! Expect to be delighted and frustrated, pleased and confused, eager and resistant, challenged and empowered—it's all part of the process of becoming a life coach.

—Mary E. Olk, Ph.D.
Licensed Psychologist
Certified Professional Coactive Coach
Professional Credentialed Coach

ACKNOWLEDGMENTS

My personal editor, Laura Kennedy, is a genius. Were it not for her patient guidance, my near-illiteracy would be apparent to the world. The proofreaders and editors at New Harbinger Publications have stewarded this book to the polished form it is today. A special thanks goes to Tesilya Hanauer at New Harbinger, who came up with the idea for this book and asked me to cocreate it with her.

The founders of the Coaches Training Institute also deserve special mention: Laura Whitworth, Henry Kimsey-House, and Karen Kimsey-House developed the core ideas of coactive coaching and created this preeminent worldwide coaching training facility. They are brilliant.

Finally, I acknowledge my partners at MyFullPractice.com: Meade Dickerson was instrumental in creating Success Coach 100, and my wife, Marla Skibbins, is my greatest support. Without her unconditional love and aliveness I would never have discovered this amazing profession. She is, always, my greatest inspiration.

INTRODUCTION

WHY I WROTE THIS BOOK

Sooner or later the ferocious dragon named Burnout rears up in front of every therapist. It took twenty years for it to happen to me, but I finally began to get tired of listening to stories of human suffering. When I discovered the profession of life coaching I thought all my prayers were answered and my career problems were over—I could use my extensive clinical experience to help mentally healthy people achieve their goals. All that and no insurance forms to fill out. Nirvana!

I soon found it wasn't that easy. Although there were definitely times when my psychotherapeutic experience came in handy, there were plenty of other times when it actually got in the way of masterful coaching. In addition to that, the whole process of marketing and promoting a successful career as a coach was remarkably different from building a therapy practice. I had to start from scratch.

Ten years ago, there weren't many therapists making the switch to coaching. Heck, there weren't many coaches, period! It was a very new field. I wish I'd had a mentor to help me through the pitfalls of my transition. Instead, I myself soon became the expert for other therapists who wanted to succeed as coaches. It was definitely a time of the blind leading the blind.

Many of us made it. But many more decided that coaching wasn't their cup of tea—or worse, loved it but couldn't make a financial go of it. This latter group—fans of coaching who couldn't find coaching clients—inspired my partners and me to start MyFullPractice.com, a Web-based training and resource center for coaches needing marketing skills. This book rose directly out of that enterprise—it's my way of mentoring you toward success as a coach. I hope this book will help you to avoid the many mistakes that I made on the journey. But more than that, I hope it will inspire you to join me in the most exciting profession on earth: life coaching.

THE HISTORY OF THE COACHING PROFESSION

The roots of coaching stretch all the way back to the pedagogical approach Plato took in his *Meno* dialogue to instruct a slave boy in geometry. Its psychological roots stem from Adler's orientation as a personal educator and Jung's encouragement of clients to do life reviews. Maslow's hierarchy of needs resonates with coaching's focus on core values while Rogers' therapeutic alliance resonates with coaching's designed alliance. However, despite these similarities, the profession of coaching as we know it evolved more from the business world than from the psychological one.

In the business world three separate streams converged to create the profession of coaching: changes in corporations' focus on training, mentoring, and staff development; the application of sports coaching to non-sports life activities; and the pioneering work of Thomas Leonard and Laura Whitworth.

As Lynn Grodzki and Wendy Allen point out in their book *The Business and Practice of Coaching* (2005), coaching emerged out of the twenty-year corporate sea change beginning in the '80s. By the end of the '90s corporations no longer envisioned themselves as traditional, stable institutions with long-term employees, formal and informal mentoring networks, and extensive in-house human resource training and development programs. Corporate focus was now multinational; employees and even managers were seen as transitory and manufacturing and service industries began migrating offshore; "outsourcing" became the buzzword.

This cost-cutting strategy created a vacuum within corporations in the areas of leadership training, management skills development, and human resource support. The separate field of executive coaching evolved to address these needs. Many of these executive coaches came from the consulting and training industries and simply added one-on-one coaching to their menu of services.

The second factor in the evolution of the coaching profession arose directly from Timothy Gallwey's book *The Inner Game of Tennis* (1997). In this book, first published in 1974, Gallwey blended psychological insights and perspectives from the human potential movement with sports coaching techniques; his book not only improved the game of tennis players around the world, it also taught tennis as a metaphor for life. Subsequently, he created Inner Game workshops and trainings for non-sports-related activities, particularly those of the business arena. In the late '80s (and even still today) corporate managers and leaders flocked to these workshops. In 1993, one of Gallwey's students, John Whitmore, extended Gallwey's metaphor and applied it directly to business settings in *Coaching for Performance* (2002).

Two coaching pioneers helped weave this wealth of disparate material into coherent coaching approaches. In 1988, Thomas Leonard, a financial advisor turned life advisor, began calling himself a coach. In 1992, he started Coach University (now Coach U) as a training center for coaches who wanted to be trained in his approach. Leonard's approach used assessment tools adapted from EST and Landmark and listening skills utilizing a Rogerian framework. He also felt a coach must be actively involved in his own development and evolution in order to coach another's growth. Practically, his style of coaching was a blend of consultation, open-ended inquiry, goal setting, and accountability. Most of the training was done on the telephone, via bridge calls in which many people could participate at the same time. These were called teleclasses.

Also in 1992, one of Leonard's colleagues—a CPA named Laura Whitworth—teamed up with one of her clients, Henry House, to create the Coaches Training Institute. An actor, House brought extensive experience as an acting coach to the enterprise. Together Whitworth and House crafted the approach of *coactive coaching*, based on the following four tenets:

1. A client is naturally creative, resourceful, and whole—not a person with a bunch of problems who needs an expert to resolve them.

2. A coach works with the whole life of the client, not just one segment (e.g., not just with the client's job challenges, financial difficulties, or health issues).

3. A coach works with the agenda a client brings to coaching; a coach doesn't just present a package of coaching tools or impose her own perspective on what the client needs.

4. Together the coach and the client design a working relationship tailored to the client's specific needs. (Whitworth, Kimsey-House, & Sandahl, 1998)

This approach extended much of humanistic psychology, the human potential movement, Lifespring, and EST into the coaching arena. Unique to the coactive coaching approach was its intensely experiential face-to-face group training and the focused individual supervision of its coach training program.

Since then, many coach training programs have sprung up. Some emphasize the more philosophical aspects of the coach-client relationship. Others focus on extensive self-development of the coach. Still others specialize in addressing the needs of a specific niche (e.g., corporate coaching, attention deficit coaching, relationship coaching, etc.).

The field of coaching is very vibrant and still changing. So far, it hasn't required state licensing, professional credentialing, or other governmental regulation. Two professional organizations that dominate the field are the International Coach Federation—a national organization that provides voluntary credentialing of coaches—and the Professional Coaches and Mentors Association—which provides coaching networks and education, primarily on the West Coast.

Today the field of coaching is still the Wild West; all you have to do is pin on a badge and call yourself the sheriff. You can spend $6,000 on professional training to be certified as a coach—or you can go down to Kinko's and print up some cards and start soliciting clients tomorrow. Or you can do both. This world of raw entrepreneurship can be shocking to many of us who have spent years of our lives—and a small fortune—to be clinically trained as therapists. It can take a while to realize that empowering mentally healthy people is a very different enterprise from treating mentally ill ones.

THE CONTENTIOUS RELATIONSHIP BETWEEN THERAPY AND COACHING

Imagine Dr. Therapy and Ms. Coaching coming into your office for a little marital counseling. There would definitely be some fireworks! Dr. Therapy would critique Ms. Coaching's lack of professionalism, laissez-faire attitude, slapdash training, and naïve cheerleading. Ms. Coaching would complain about Dr. Therapy's rigidity, pessimistic attitude, repressed stuffiness, and tendency to see psychopathology everywhere.

After their venting, deeper issues would emerge. Turns out Dr. Therapy resents Ms. Coaching's easier lifestyle and more positive cash flow—coaching on the telephone from her home, she's earning twice as much as he is. This challenges Dr. Therapy's self-image and brings up questions about his self-worth. Meanwhile, Ms. Coaching's surface optimism actually masks a feeling of inferiority and a deep-seated fear that she might end up in over her head with some of her clients.

Can this marriage be saved? That question is as yet unanswered. Controversy about this very topic continues in professional journals, trade magazines, and graduate school classes across the country. Therapists tend to minimize the accomplishments of coaching, while coaches tend to turn therapists into caricatures painted with Freudian features. Neither really understands what the other is up to.

At the same time, some coaches are masterful at sending mentally ill clients to therapists for psychological support. And some therapists—particularly those working with attention-deficit disorders—team very effectively with coaches. There's hope for a peaceful resolution to this conflict. As a practitioner in both worlds, you will be pioneering reconciliation between these two camps. I hope this book will help you with that task.

ABOUT THE AUTHOR

I received my Ph.D. in clinical psychology decades ago from the Professional School of Psychology at San Francisco, and have practiced in residential treatment centers and addiction treatment centers as well as privately. I've also taught in three graduate psychology programs and supervised therapists. I loved my years as a psychotherapist.

I love my new career as a coach just as much. I have my own private coaching practice (www.insightorientedcoaching.com) and was the founding coordinator of the Life Coaching Certificate Program, a continuing education certificate program at the John F. Kennedy University in Pleasant Hill, California (www.jfku.edu). I'm a senior supervisor of student coaches at the Coaches Training Institute in San Rafael. I'm also one of three founders of MyFullPractice. com, a Web site that supports coaches in marketing and building their coaching practice (www.myfullpractice.com).

HOW TO USE THIS BOOK

This book is organized to appeal both to readers who like to randomly jump all over a book and to those who like to read from page one to the end. Initially we'll concentrate on learning the specific tools coaches use, and we'll explore how to adapt your current skills to this new venue (chapters 1 through 3). Then we'll look at the the differences between therapy and coaching (chapter 4). We'll next take a closer look at the unique way coaching addresses human issues (chapter 5) and then discuss a typical coaching session as well as typical intake and sample sessions (chapters 6 through 8). We'll then apply these principles and practices to you as a fledgling coach, so that you can take them on a test drive and use your own life as a case study (chapter 9). The focus will then shift to more practical concerns: legal, ethical, and administrative issues in coaching, creating a workable business plan to launch your coaching practice, attracting coaching clients, and ensuring a steady flow of continuing business (chapters 10 through 13).

Go to what you need or read the book from cover to cover—either way, you can successfully prepare yourself for life as a coach. Let's get started!

CHAPTER ONE

EMBARKING ON THE JOURNEY

Twenty percent of therapists have either already added coaching to their repertoire, or are contemplating doing so. Since you've picked up this book, you're probably considering joining this group. Congratulations! Coaching is one of the most exciting adventures in the human services realm.

But what exactly is coaching? Many therapists wonder, "How is coaching different from what I already do?" Others comment, "I haven't the slightest idea how I would even begin to start a coaching practice."

This workbook arose in response to these laments. By the time you've finished reading the chapters and doing the exercises of this book, you will have already launched your career as a coach.

In the next chapter a lot of coaching skills will be introduced. But let's introduce the first coaching skill early, in the service of you moving toward success as a coach:

COACHING SKILL: Envisioning a Future Outcome

Goal: When a client begins to vividly describe a possible future, he also begins to orient his actions toward it. A fleshed-out vision will pull a client toward it. The client will begin to see paths around obstacles, keeping his eyes on the prize rather than focusing on difficulties that lie in the way.

Tool: Take the client into a successful future; then ask questions to help the client powerfully visualize this intended future scenario.

Apply this tool to yourself: close your eyes for a moment and imagine you're on your way to becoming a highly successful coach as well as a psychotherapist. Seriously, close those eyes, even if just for a second. See and feel your experience. Congratulations! Now read on …

Let's jump ahead to a couple of months in the future. Thanks to your hard work you've now successfully embarked on your coaching career. Let's see what you have accomplished in these first few months:

TEN THINGS YOU HAVE LEARNED FROM THIS BOOK

1. You can now speak clearly about the differences between coaching and therapy.

2. You can differentiate between clients who can benefit from coaching and clients who may need psychotherapy.

3. You're clear about what kind of person you're looking for as a potential coaching client.

4. You know how to apply the strengths and tools you already have as a therapist to your coaching practice.

5. You have learned new coaching tools and applied them to your work.

6. You have learned how to self-coach to achieve the goals you desire in life.

7. You know how to avoid the possible ethical, professional, and legal pitfalls and complications that could arise from blending a coaching practice with a psycho-therapy practice.

8. You've created a business plan for your coaching practice tailored to your specific circumstances, with clear guidelines on how to succeed.

9. You've begun a marketing campaign to attract potential coaching clients.

10. You're promoting your coaching practice in a way that capitalizes on your strengths, and avoids forcing you to do things you don't want to do.

Nice job on your accomplishments! Not a bad list … Now here is an exercise to help set you on this path:

BEGINNING WITH THE GOAL IN SIGHT

1. In a couple of sentences, describe the ideal career outcome you'll achieve from reading this book.

2. Describe what changes will occur in you to make you an excellent and successful coach.

3. Imagine yourself two months into the future; what do you have now that you didn't have when you started reading this book?

Now let's start taking the steps necessary to get you from where you are to success as a coach. We'll start with answering that perplexing question: What the heck is coaching anyway?

CHAPTER TWO

THE BASIC SKILLS OF COACHING

What the heck is coaching anyway? Have you ever noticed how one question leads to others? From that one coaching question, three related questions immediately spin off:

✓ What are the guiding principles of coaching?

✓ Why do people go to coaching?

✓ What are the key skills a coach needs?

WHAT ARE THE GUIDING PRINCIPLES OF COACHING?

The International Coach Federation—the largest professional organization of coaches—answers this question best on its website (www.coachfederation.org):

Professional Coaching is an ongoing professional relationship that helps people produce extraordinary results in their lives, careers, businesses, or organizations. Through the process of coaching, clients deepen their learning, improve their performance, and enhance their quality of life. In each meeting, the client chooses the focus of conversation, while the coach listens and contributes observations and questions. This interaction creates clarity and moves the client into action. Coaching accelerates the client's progress by providing greater focus and awareness of choice. Coaching concentrates on where clients are now and what they are willing to do to get where they want to be in the future, recognizing that results are a matter of the client's intentions, choices and actions, supported by the coach's efforts and application of the coaching process.

The International Coach Federation adheres to a form of coaching that honors the client as the expert in his/her life and work and believes that every client is creative, resourceful, and whole. Standing on this foundation, the coach's responsibility is to:

- Discover, clarify, and align with what the client wants to achieve
- Encourage client self-discovery
- Elicit client-generated solutions and strategies
- Hold the client responsible and accountable

There are many paths to these goals. Some schools of coaching encourage coaches to take almost a mentorship role with clients, to act as expert guides. Other schools, founded in the belief that clients are expert at solving their own problems, teach coaches strategies to unleash the genius of clients. Most coaches blend these approaches.

WHY DO PEOPLE GO TO COACHING?

People often end up in therapy because internal pain and external stress have become unmanageable. They go to therapy because nothing else has worked. People go to coaching for very different reasons.

Most clients enter coaching on their own initiative. They come to it with excitement and anticipation. They've heard enthusiastic reports about the impact of coaching and want to try it themselves. Many of them have specific projects they want to move forward (new career, promotion, retirement). Others may seek more balance in their life or may simply be hungry for new possibilities. Coaching clients are motivated to change because they want a richer life, not because they're in pain. Sometimes, employees in corporations will be assigned a coach to address poor job performance. But most of these folks, too, are open to coaching.

Coaching clients come from all walks of life and backgrounds; they may be artists, social entrepreneurs working in nonprofits, managers, salespeople, CEOs, or employees who have been recently laid off. Most want to work on their careers, but may also want coaching on issues around personal relationships with family, friends, and intimate partners.

The chief feature of coaching clients that distinguishes them from therapy clients is that coaching clients are, for the most part, mentally healthy individuals. Whatever self-limiting beliefs, habits, and patterns they may have, these factors aren't so severe that they affect a client's ability to function effectively in the world. Fundamental to coaching is accepting that the world is populated with remarkable, mature, mentally healthy adults.

However, after working as a psychotherapist, one tends to see psychopathology everywhere. I vividly remember one afternoon when I worked at a residential treatment center for schizophrenic adolescents. Five staff took seven kids to the beach for an outing. We were all very busy—prying kids off rocks, holding onto them while they screamed, defusing rock-throwing fits—when, unexpectedly, we witnessed an amazing event.

A teacher walked onto the beach. Behind her, in single file, was a line of fifteen students. When she got to the water she blew a whistle. The kids then broke rank and went to play at the other end of the beach from our eccentric charges. Meanwhile, the teacher sat down and read a book. Finally she got up and blew her whistle a second time. The students promptly lined back up and off they marched.

We were all stunned. After years of working in residential treatment we had completely forgotten how typical kids looked and acted. When, as a coach, you realize how many healthy adults there are in the world, eager to grow and develop, you, too, will be amazed.

WHAT ARE THE KEY SKILLS A COACH NEEDS?

The following is a brief overview of essential coaching skills; the tools you use to implement these skills will be explored in greater depth in the next chapter.

The Ability to Ask Questions

A coach needs a strong curiosity and the ability to ask questions that will help clients explore the circumstances of their present life and map a path to a future of their own design. You could distill almost every coaching session down to three questions:

1. What do you want?

2. How are you going to get it?

3. How will I, as your coach, know that you've gotten it?

Laser Articulation

A coach also needs *laser articulation*—a strong ability to speak to the essence of the material the client sets as the agenda for the coaching session. The biggest hurdle therapists-turned-coaches face is that they talk too much. As a supervisor, I often have my student coaches follow the *two sentence rule* for a week. This is a simple—but not easy—exercise. There are only two elements to the two sentence rule:

1.   The coach is only allowed to speak two sentences at a time.

2.   The coach's second sentence must be a question.

Practicing the two sentence rule helps develop the muscle of self-management—a muscle that needs to be strong to learn to "Shut up and coach!"

The Ability to Create Accountability

A coach also needs to be able to create and maintain accountable environments in which clients can determine the next step toward their goals, celebrate achieving goals, and make adjustments to strategies when goals aren't successfully achieved.

Coaching homework must be specific, measurable, and reported back to the coach. Homework that focuses on taking action in the world is preferable to homework oriented to thinking, planning, contemplating, or imagining. "Just do it!" is a strong coaching motto.

The Ability to Provide Support

A coach also needs to be able to give clients the support and acknowledgment necessary to help them overcome any self-sabotaging beliefs that could interfere with the achievement of their goals.

When offering acknowledgments, it's essential to include a question after you have made the acknowledgment, something like, "I'm wondering if you took in what I just said. What's going on over there in you right now?" Unfortunately, most of us usually duck away from acknowledgments. It can embarrass us to hear someone comment on our excellent qualities and achievements. As coaches, we must stop clients from shrugging off praise, and instead, help them to really experience being seen and respected. Often just this intervention alone can change a client's life.

INFORMATIONAL INTERVIEWS

Now it's your turn to discover how coaches grapple with the deadly question "What is a coach?" Go to the International Coach Federation Website (www.coachfederation.org). From their directory of coaches, choose three coaches who look like they would be good to talk to about coaching. Pick folks with life experiences similar to yours.

Here are some questions you might want to ask them:

Why did you choose coaching as a profession?

What did you learn from transitioning to coaching from your previous profession?

What coaching skills do you think are most important?

What training do you recommend for coaches just starting out?

What's the hardest part of being a coach?

What do you love the most about being a coach?

What advice do you have for me?

Next, summarize what you've learned from each coach:

Coach number one:

Coach number two:

Coach number three:

CHAPTER THREE

ADAPTING THE TOOLS YOU ALREADY HAVE

On the path to becoming masterful coaches, therapists have many things going for them. As therapists, our training and experience have given us five skill sets that stand us in good stead in our drive to succeed as coaches: listening/questioning, empathy, articulation/clarification, structuring/goal setting, and superego management. Let's see how these skills can be adapted to the coaching setting.

LISTENING/QUESTIONING

The skills of listening and questioning are at the heart of both therapy and coaching. By listening actively and questioning in an open-ended manner, both therapists and coaches create a space for clients to reflect on their choices, desires, obstacles, patterns, and dreams. Both therapy and coaching provide the space to consider the core questions of life: Who am I? How did I get to where I am? Where am I going? What do I want? How do I get what I want? What gets in the way of getting what I want? Why am I here?

For the psychotherapist working with a deeply disturbed client, structure and support are necessary to help the client address these questions in a healthy manner. A mentally healthy client, on the other hand, enjoys the challenge of tackling these questions bluntly and directly. This is what makes coaching so exciting.

As therapists, we already know the difference between questions that elicit monosyllabic responses and questions that promote deeper exploration on the part of the client. We have already seen how much more productive open-ended questions are. We have also already learned to follow the thread of a client's story, gently probing when necessary and being silent when receptivity alone is needed. We have learned how to hang out in that open, inviting space that Freud called "evenly suspended attention." As therapists, our listening and questioning skills have already been woven into a rich tapestry.

One difference between therapy and coaching is the use of these listening and questioning skills. Although the skills are similar, the focus shifts. In therapy, the focus may include exploring dysfunctional patterns of behavior, self-negating beliefs, historical roots of these patterns and beliefs, and the resolution of these into functional behavior and positive, self-affirming beliefs. In coaching, the focus is on examining current values, goals, and dreams—and discovering the future steps necessary to live these values more fully, achieve these goals, and realize these dreams.

A particular kind of question can be problematic in therapy and even more so in coaching. This is the *why?* question. Some why questions are therapeutically very valuable. Insight-oriented therapy is essentially grounded in why questions. A core premise of such therapy is that once you understand the origins of your beliefs and behaviors you can begin to change them.

However, why questions can also be perceived negatively. A psychiatrist I once worked with annoyed all of his colleagues by answering any question about himself that contained the word "why" with "Because I am fat, ugly, stupid, lazy, or crazy." He did this because he believed that almost all why questions can be perceived as veiled judgments on the part of the questioner. We can see this easily with a question like "Why did you leave the cap off the toothpaste?" But it can also be true with questions like "Why did you do that?" or "Why were you late to the appointment?" Every question has the potential to be perceived as an attack; why questions seem to be even more highly charged in this regard, infantilizing the client—whether inadvertently or purposely—and making her defensive.

Strongly authoritarian-based coaches also utilize why questions. The authoritarian approach is to help a client find out why he is failing to get the results he desires and then change his strategy. The premise behind using why questions is that clients need education and direction, and eliciting resistance in the course of straightening a client out is acceptable.

For empowerment-based coaches, the origins of a situation are of little interest. They are more likely to use open-ended questions that contain words like "when," "how," "where," or "with whom." These types of questions invite a more nondefensive exploration of possibilities.

Let's see what you can discover about the differences between your own therapy-based questioning and coaching-based questioning. Again, if you haven't coached before, use your imagination.

TWO TYPES OF QUESTIONING

1. Make a list of the kinds of questions you typically ask in therapy.

2. Make a list of questions you imagine might be useful as a coach.

3. What differences do you notice?

Both therapists and coaches ask *impact questions*—questions that change people's lives. In coaching, however, impact questions take a particular form. The following is a list of questions coaches typically use, in no particular order:

Opening question: What would you like to focus on today?

Positive future orientation: What would your life be like if this were handled?

Skills exploration: Who do you have to be in order to deal with this issue skillfully?

Skills exploration: What strengths do you have within you to deal with this issue?

Skills exploration: What resources do you have around you to deal with this issue?

Opening new perspectives: What are some other ways of looking at this situation?

Reframing: What if this weren't a problem—what else might it be?

Using creativity: What metaphor (or image, or picture) can you imagine that expresses this issue?

Call to action: How will you deal with this issue?

Planning: What do you need in order to go on from here?

Planning: How will you get what you need?

Planning and accountability: What's the next step?

Planning and accountability: When will you take the next step?

Planning and accountability: How will I know you took this step?

COACHING SKILL: Asking Impact Questions

Goal: In coaching, an impact question accomplishes three things:

1. It gets the client to look deeply into his direct experience or positive future.

2. It invites further investigation on the part of the client—without subtly imposing the focus or interest of the coach onto the exploration of the client.

3. It opens up new possibilities.

Tool: Craft almost every question you ask so that rather than gathering data or examining problems, barriers, or past history, questions invite further exploration. For example, instead of asking "What is your salary?" ask "How do you feel about your salary?"

CASE EXAMPLE: THERAPEUTIC VS. COACHING QUESTIONS

Let's look at the difference between therapeutic and coaching questions. In the following scenario the client is stuck, feeling powerless, trapped in a set of circumstances. First let's look at some typical questions a therapist might ask:

How does it feel to be stuck?

What time in your past does this remind you of?

Have you ever seen this pattern before?

Tell me more about that.

Does this remind you of anyone in your family?

How did your parents (or mother/father) handle being stuck?

How do you want to handle it differently from the way they did?

How do you want to handle this differently from how you have previously handled being stuck?

What are you going to have to change to handle things differently?

Now let's look at the questions a coach might ask in the same situation:

Tell me about this stuck place.

If it were a painting, what would it look like?

What would being unstuck look like?

What would the painting of unstuck look like?

What do you notice when you compare those two paintings?

How is being stuck the perfect place for you right now?

What judgments do you have about being stuck?

What would stuck feel like if you stopped judging yourself for being there?

What can you learn from being stuck?

If this is the right time to move beyond stuck, how are you going to do that?

If this is a good time to stay stuck, how are you going to defend yourself against judgments?

I can hear you saying that, as therapists, you've often used the questions I've labeled coaching questions. However, if you read both lists you can see there's a difference in intent behind the two sets of questions. The first set encourages the client to become more insightful about her situation. The second set fosters the client's living in either an unstuck place or a place of full, nonjudgmental acceptance of the stuckness.

EMPATHY

As therapists, our clinical clients are often surprised at how well we're able to intuit what's going on for them. We have finely honed our capacity to read the cues in our clients' posture, gesture, tone, and word choices. It can seem like we have a sixth sense; actually, of course, it's just a highly attuned understanding of the other, arising from years of experience and education.

When I first heard that most coaching was done on the telephone I was worried. I was afraid that it would leave me blind in some way—that, not being face-to-face, I would be missing a major source of information about my client. I thought relying on voice alone would be a severe handicap.

I was very wrong. It's remarkable how well skills at reading the energy of a client can operate over the phone. I've found that even with clients halfway across the globe, whom I've never met face-to-face, I'm just as accurate in my intuitions and my capacity to empathize over the phone as in person.

The fact that in phone coaching neither the client nor the coach has to make eye contact carries two additional bonuses: it promotes authenticity on the part of the client because he doesn't have to expend energy on image management, and it frees the coach to take whatever notes necessary without fear of breaking contact with the client.

ARTICULATION/CLARIFICATION

The reflective listening skills we practice in psychotherapy translate easily to coaching. In therapy it can be very powerful for clients to hear their own words fed back to them. Equally powerful can be the succinct summation of a theme, the articulation of a dynamic or pattern we see, or the clarification of an issue which has seemed clouded to the client. This skill of reflective listening combines careful listening, distilling the material to its essential elements, and feeding it back in a language the client understands.

When free from analysis, interpretation, and abstraction, reflective listening can also be an elegant coaching interaction. However, eliminating these elements from our reflective listening takes real commitment. The trick is to practice reflective listening without any helpful hidden agenda or suppressed insight of our own. Instead, it must be practiced from the place of someone seeking to better understand the client. Also, rather than simply demonstrating the expertise of the coach's listening skills, reflective listening is often the prelude to asking an impact question.

COACHING SKILL: Laser Articulation

Goal: Occasionally the coach can wrap up an issue presented by the client into a clear, brief concept; this can make the issue more accessible for the client to talk about.

Tool: Speak in one (or at most two) sentences to the essence of the particular issue the client is bringing to coaching.

CASE EXAMPLE: THERAPEUTIC ARTICULATION VS. LASER ARTICULATION

Client:	"I'm under a whole lot of stress right now. My boss keeps piling on assignments and just doesn't seem to hear me when I say I can't handle any more. And the crew I'm supervising keeps screwing up. Then I have to go in and fix their mistakes rather than handling my assignment. I'm getting fried."
The therapist might say:	"It sounds like you're feeling unable to control everything, and yet at the same time you're expected to."
The coach might say:	"So, work sucks. What do you need?"

STRUCTURING/GOAL SETTING

Training in cognitive-based therapies also provides a strong foundation for key coaching tools in structuring and goal setting. The process of creating goals and setting up step-by-step, phase-by-phase programs for attaining all the smaller milestones necessary to complete the goal is the meat and potatoes of cognitive work.

This skill is invaluable for a coach. Much of the work of coaching is the creation of micro-goals in the service of a more long-term destination. A question commonly asked in coaching is, "What specific task can you complete this week to take one step toward achieving your goal?"

Both the goal-trained therapist and the goal-oriented coach also know how important it is to acknowledge and celebrate the small victories along the path. Clients often want to minimize small successes and focus instead on the next Herculean task. We have to teach them to stop for a moment to relish their accomplishments before rushing off to the next challenge. Therapeutic experience in this is excellent training for doing the same thing as a coach.

COACHING SKILL: Assigning Impact Homework

Goal: In therapy, much of the impact comes from the direct interactions between therapist and client. In coaching, most of the impact comes from the client trying new behaviors, perspectives, and strategies. Assigning life-changing homework between sessions is essential to impactful coaching.

Tool: Assign the client an action to be accomplished that is specific, doable, measurable, and reportable.

CASE EXAMPLE: COACHING HOMEWORK

The fried client from the previous example realized that she needed to clarify her job assignment from her supervisor. To support this, the coach assigned homework. The homework wasn't "Spend this week thinking about how you would like your job to be." Such an assignment isn't specific, measurable, or reportable. Instead the coach assigned something a little different:

Coach: "Okay, here's your homework: this week, write up a memo of your understanding of your job description. Then send it to your supervisor and request a meeting to clarify whether your perception matches his. Will you do that?"

Client: "Yes."

Coach: "How will I know it's been done?"

Client: "I'll send you a copy of the job description e-mail that I send him, and—if we can schedule the meeting before my next coaching session—I'll report back then on how it went."

Coach: "Great! I love your boldness at taking this on!"

SUPEREGO MANAGEMENT

Regardless of our theoretical foundations, as therapists we've all had to address the self-destructive beliefs, internal monologues, and counterproductive behaviors of clients. Call it what you will—the superego, the inner judge, the parental introject, negative self-esteem, habitualized self-defeating behavioral patterns, interference from the lateral prefrontal cortex of the brain— we all have to deal with it. It's an intrapsychic force that works against the course of therapeutic growth. As therapists, we already have extensive experience in supporting clients in challenging these negative beliefs.

Coaches call this critical inner voice the Gremlin or the Saboteur. In coaching, the historical origins of self-defeating and self-attacking behavior aren't of much interest—coaches just want to get the behavior out of the way, so the client can make forward progress.

The capacity of a client to turn down the volume on this critical inner voice is a good litmus test of the client's suitability for coaching. Mentally healthy people can learn the self-management skills needed to turn down the volume of this voice and readily move it out of their way. Clients who are unable to stop these self-attacks may be better suited for a stint of psycho-therapy. (Please note, I do not recommend acting as both therapist and coach for a client; see chapter 10 for more on legal, administrative, and ethical issues.)

COACHING SKILL: Dealing with the Gremlin

Goal: The language of *Taming Your Gremlin: A Guide to Enjoying Yourself* by Richard Carson and Novle Rogers (1990) has been adopted by many coaches working with the critical inner voices of clients; the objective is to circumvent or diminish the effect of these voices on the client's capacity to move forward in life.

Tool: Use either circumambulation or confrontation to turn down the volume of the superego judge. *Circumambulation* involves coaching around the superego by focusing on the future rather than attacking the critical voice directly; confrontation involves addressing the critical voice directly and removing it from the coaching interaction.

CASE EXAMPLE: DEALING WITH THE GREMLIN

The client is a freelance journalist who specializes in articles about American history.

Client: "I've got writer's block. Every time I sit down to finish my essay my inner voice tells me how trite it is, how superficial my thinking sounds, and how arrogant I am to think it could ever be published."

Using Circumambulation (go to a value, a vision, or a future scenario that is more compelling than the current inner judgment):

Coach: "Imagine your agent is calling you to congratulate you for getting your piece in *The New Yorker*. You're talking to her and telling her how you got over the pesky writer's block you had writing this article. What do you say to her?"

Using Confrontation (give the inner critical voice a name, an image, and then devise a strategy for defusing it):

The client has already identified his critical voice as Judge Isaac Parker, the hanging judge of Arkansas in the 1880s.

Coach: "We know this critter, don't we? It's old Judge Parker coming to do you in. Looks like he's got you hamstrung, and he's tightening the noose around your neck. What are you going to do?"

Client laughs: "Wait, I've got a pardon right here from President Grover Cleveland. Set this man free!"

Coach: "Okay, so now you've got the pardon. What do you need to tell Judge Parker?"

Client: "Take a vacation, judge. You need to lighten up a little. Leave me alone."

Coach: "What do you need to keep the judge off your back?"

Client: "Actually, I have a copy of a real presidential pardon by President Cleveland in my files. I think I'll mount it over my desk."

Coach: "I love it!"

One of the biggest gremlins that many therapeutically trained coaches will have to face themselves is the voice that says, "I don't know anything about business—or weather forecasting or brain surgery or whatever profession this client practices—how can I help this person?" It's quite a transition to go from the role of therapist as expert to a place of inexperience and ignorance. It's hard on the old ego.

What you have to do is patiently remind your own scared inner voice that you don't need to know how to do the client's job. As a coach, all you need is to trust that the client will be able to figure out what to do, and inquire with the client about what's next.

A STRONG FOUNDATION

As a therapist, regardless of the nature of your training—psychodynamic, narrative, cognitive, humanistic, transpersonal, or transactional—you've already mastered many coaching skills. To celebrate this achievement, fill out the following worksheet.

THE COACHING SKILLS ASSESSMENT SHEET: EXISTING SKILLS

Make a list of at least five skills you already possess that you can use in coaching. Under each skill make a note of how you may need to modify this clinical skill for the coaching relationship, based on what you have learned in this and previous chapters.

1.

2.

3.

4.

5.

6.

7.

Identifying the skills and abilities that a client possesses is a great asset for both client and coach. You can use the following skills assessment sheet with your clients:

SKILLS ASSESSMENT SHEET: EXISTING SKILLS

Make a list of at least five skills you already possess that you can use in working with the situation you are facing. Under each skill, make a note on how you may need to modify this existing skill to your new situation.

1.

2.

3.

4.

5.

6.

7.

Now let's see how you measure up in terms of using the skills articulated in this chapter:

THE COACHING SKILLS ASSESSMENT SHEET: CORE SKILLS ASSESSMENT

On a scale of 1 to 10, rate yourself in terms of your familiarity with the coaching skills discussed in this chapter. A score of 1 means you don't have a clue how to use the skill; a 5 means you have some familiarity and expertise with using the skill; a 10 means you have mastered the skill.

Skill Score

Asking impact questions:

Laser articulation:

Assigning impact homework:

Dealing with the Gremlin using circumambulation:

Dealing with the Gremlin using confrontation:

What's your plan for raising these scores?

CHAPTER FOUR

DIFFERENCES BETWEEN THERAPY & COACHING

Now that we've looked at the history of coaching, as well as some of the skills, tools, and principles that coaching involves, let's get back to that pesky question "What the heck is coaching anyway?" In this chapter, we'll refine our definition of coaching down to its essential qualities.

If you put twenty coaches in a room and ask them what coaching is, you'll get twenty different definitions. I did exactly that. Let's look at ten of these definitions:

"Coaches help you achieve your full potential."

"Coaching helps you improve your performance in your professional and personal life."

"Coaching empowers you to change your life."

"A coach can help you overcome obstacles to achieving your goals and actualizing your dreams."

"Coaching assists you in defining your goals and designing a plan to achieve them—and then holds you accountable to your plan."

"Coaching is an interpersonal technology that helps you get from where you are to where you want to be."

"Corporate coaches work within a corporate culture to help individuals and teams create exceptional results."

"Business coaches help executives, managers, and line staff become leaders and innovators in the workplace."

"Coaching is therapy for mentally healthy people."

"Coaching helps you make your dreams come true."

And there are many more. As I sifted through these diverse perspectives, four common themes began to emerge:

- ✓ Coaching is about moving from the present toward a future that the client designs.

- ✓ Coaching focuses more on how to get there than on what's in the way.

- ✓ The role of the coach is to empower the client.

- ✓ Coaching is practical, straightforward, and optimistic.

As practicing therapists as well as coaches, we must delineate the differences between what we do when we coach and what we do when we act as therapists. Let's look at therapy. In my opinion, the following four themes seem to be true for all forms of psychotherapy:

- ✓ Psychotherapy is grounded in the perspective that some pattern, behavior, belief, habit, or dynamic is keeping the client from achieving all the client wants out of life.

- ✓ It is possible—through insight, testing, learning new behavior, adaptation, training, or recontextualizing—for the client to attain a more functional way of acting and being.

- ✓ The role of the therapist is to help the client through this transition.

- ✓ The therapist utilizes extensive training in psychological theory and clinical application to achieve this goal.

DIFFERENTIATING BETWEEN THERAPY & COACHING

When a roomful of coaches starts comparing therapy and coaching, some obvious differences emerge:

Therapy	Coaching
Therapy is about what's holding you back.	Coaching is about knowing where you're headed.
A therapy client needs help with a specific problem.	A coaching client wants to achieve a specific goal.
A therapist is a highly trained professional employing tools from the science of psychology to implement a treatment plan.	A coach is a generalist who relies less on expertise and more on trust in the inherent capacity of clients to solve their own problems.

Of course, a great deal of the territories of these two overlap. Both enterprises rely extensively on listening, questioning, acknowledging, clarifying, goal setting, nonjudgmental acceptance, and self-management. That's why, on learning about coaching, so many therapists say, "Well, that's what I'm already doing!" In the last chapter we looked in depth at important therapeutic skills that transfer to coaching. Here we're trying to clarify the difference between therapy and coaching.

If we distilled this difference down to its essential elements, they would look something like this: therapy involves the implementation of a treatment plan with the help and guidance of a trained therapist, to help a client resolve a life problem; coaching involves the design of a life plan and specific goals within that plan—as well as the week-to-week accountable environment necessary to achieving these goals—with the support of a coach who trusts the client to succeed.

Let's see what distinctions you can find between these two endeavors:

YOUR CURRENT PRACTICE

1. In a few sentences, define the kind of psychotherapy you currently practice.

2. Make a short list of the types of client problems you commonly work with.

3. In your own words, distinguish between therapy and coaching.

What do you notice about the similarities and differences between what you're currently doing and coaching? Another way to tease out the differences between the two is to look at the differences between coaching clients and therapy clients. The following exercise asks you to visualize the kind of client you'll work with as a coach. This is a common coaching approach: envisioning the future as already in existence. Use your imagination.

THE DEFINING YOUR IDEAL CLIENTELE EXERCISE

1. In a few sentences, describe your typical therapy client. (What led her to therapy? What does she want from therapy?)

2. In a few sentences, describe your ideal coaching client. (What led him to coaching? What does he want from coaching?)

So, now that you have an idea of the kind of people you'll serve as a coach, let's return to our central issue: distinguishing between therapy and coaching. We can sum up the differences we've observed thus: therapy focuses on resolving a client's problems and coaching focuses on achieving the client's aims. So, now that this distinction is clear, how do you describe what exactly coaching is? Here's where things start to get complicated again.

COACHING & LOCUS OF CONTROL

Linguist Benjamin Whorf (1964) suggested that the Eskimo people have more names for snow than Europeans because they need to differentiate between the different kinds of snow in order to survive. Similarly, therapists have dozens of names for therapy, to help differentiate their work from that of other therapists. Coaching, a young discipline, has just the one general name for the profession. Although sometimes it's called "life coaching" or "executive coaching," there is nothing like the diversity you see in names for different therapy styles. This is both unfortunate and confusing; a number of different—and sometimes conflicting—approaches fall under this one rubric of coaching. However, we can sort these approaches along a continuum of authority. Work on *locus of control* has taught us that there is a range of perceived autonomy in human interactions. This is also true in coaching.

On one extreme, all authority is placed in the hands of the coach. One popular coach said, "If my client doesn't do what I tell him to do, I fire him!" I call this extreme the *coach-as-manager*. In this role, the coach is seen as the unquestioned authority on what needs to be done. The coach provides the blueprint for action and makes sure her rules are followed. The client has a very limited locus of control and looks to the coach for guidance.

Many managers are being given coach training these days. The role of coach and the role of manager are so diametrically different that such training can leave people confused. One manager said to me, "I don't get it. As a coach I'm supposed to support the dreams of my employee, but as a manager I have to fire him if he doesn't perform. That's quite a stretch." If a manager takes the coach-as-manager position it might not be such a stretch. However, many coaches question whether such a controlling stance can really be called coaching. After all, coaches don't hire and fire, yet managers must. Moreover, a manager can't maintain confidentiality, neutrality, or unconditional support of a client if it will result in dire consequences to the company's bottom line.

In the middle of this continuum, between authoritarianism and egalitarianism, is the *coach-as-consultant*. The coach-as-consultant may have additional expertise in communication skills, strategic planning, financial analysis, emotional intelligence, or some other area. In this role, the coach provides advice, support, and brainstorming to help clients advance toward their goals. The coach's wealth of life experience and professional experience is made available to the client.

On the egalitarian end of the continuum lies the *coach-as-empowerer*. The coach-as-empowerer believes that the elements a client needs to resolve any challenge *already exist inside the psyche of the client*. The coach-as-empowerer takes the lead from the client, and provides no additional expertise, no advice, no suggestions. The locus of control rests completely with the client. The coach operates from total confidence and trust in the talents and genius of the client. The role of the coach is to help clients clarify their goals; the coach-as-empowerer asks questions that help clients create the steps necessary to achieve these goals, holds the client accountable for taking these steps, and celebrates little victories along the way. As goals change—or are achieved—the coach-as-empowerer stays curious about what comes next.

Now, most of you reading this have probably already deduced my opinion about what the role of the coach should be. I firmly believe that this last form of coaching—empowerment coaching—is not only best suited to therapists, but is also best suited to the healthy, mature coaching clients that we serve. Much of this book reflects this opinion.

However, which coaching style you embrace is up to you. In a way it's like choosing your specialty as a therapist. You wouldn't do family sculpture, biofeedback, narrative therapy, dream work, psychodynamic psychotherapy, behavior modification, and art therapy with the same schizophrenic adolescent. You must choose the niche and style that best suits your temperament, training, and philosophy of life.

Now let's take a look at how these three approaches differ:

CASE EXAMPLE: THREE COACHING POSITIONS

Scenario: The client comes on the call upset that her husband keeps belittling her work. He wants her to stop being an entrepreneur and get a regular paying job.

Coach-as-manager: "I think you need to just sit down with him and have a good heart-to-heart. Show him the numbers we worked out about your potential earnings as an entrepreneur compared with those you'd make at some dead-end job. He'll come to see this is in his best interests, too."

Coach-as-consultant: "I faced a similar challenge early in my coaching career. What worked for me was to design an alliance with my partner. He told me what he needed and wanted financially, and I told him what I needed and wanted in terms of support from him in building my business. The two of us found a place of compromise we both could live with. What are your thoughts about having that kind of conversation with your husband?"

Coach-as-empowerer: "That sounds really frustrating. What's your plan for dealing with him?"

Let's see where you place yourself on this continuum:

CONTRASTING THERAPY & COACHING: DIFFERENT LEVELS OF AUTHORITY

1.   Where in the following continuum do you place your work as a psychotherapist?

Usually clearly direct the client.	Usually consult with the client.	Usually let the client direct the work.

2.   Where in the following continuum do you imagine placing your work as a coach?

Usually clearly direct the client.	Usually consult with the client.	Usually let the client direct the work.

Some elements are common to all three of these approaches; for example, goal setting and accountability. One key practical difference, however, is that as coaching shifts from authoritarian to egalitarian, more self-management is needed on the part of the coach. Self-management in this case means restraining yourself from telling the client what to do and not sharing all the insights, assessments, or interpretations you may have.

It's fairly easy to know all the answers and tell the client what to do. Working as a consultant with your client requires more flexibility—and therefore more self-management. You're suggesting rather than telling. But to give up the role of expert completely, to see the source of all expertise as in the client, requires a great deal of self-management and trust. Most of us in the helping professions are quite attached to our identification as expert helpers and are reluctant to give that up, even in the service of empowering our clients. It can be hard to discard your brilliance.

At first glance it may appear that the coach-as-consultant role is the best fit for a therapist looking to become a coach. After all, as therapists we have years of training in human communications, systems theory, psychodynamics, and behavioral change. We are preeminent experts in these areas. It would be a shame to give up all that hard-won expertise.

However, I suggest you do precisely that. You need to give up your authority as an expert in psychology. Here are two reasons why:

Experts Can't Be Trusted

Many mentally healthy clients distrust therapists. And not unreasonably—all our training in psychology has warped our point of view. We are experts in the assessment and treatment of psychopathology. And so we tend to see it everywhere: everyone is neurotic, corporations are dysfunctional, the government is addicted to power and control.

Most people are mentally healthy. Until you wrap your mind around that fact you'll be re-creating your clinical practice wherever you go. You'll be unconsciously disempowering your clients by finding problems they need to solve. They'll sense that you don't completely trust them, that you regard them as patients. You may get compliance or you may get rebellion—both of which are expressions of dissatisfaction at being regarded as somehow defective. You can't truly coach from a one-up position.

The Wrong Tool for the Job

It's inappropriate to apply a therapeutic perspective to most real-life situations, especially work settings. Therapeutic perspectives are well-honed tools that are invaluable in assisting dysfunctional clients to become functional, but they are simply inadequate for addressing the dynamics of already functional environments. Of course, this hasn't stopped psychodynamic and psychologically based systems theorists from analyzing the workplace. Indeed, these ideas have been elegantly applied to the workplace for years—with no apparent impact on work environments whatsoever. Pointing out the narcissistic qualities of leadership, analyzing top-down communication flow patterns, and discoursing on parentified employer-employee relationships have all fallen on deaf ears. Having twenty-three names for snow doesn't help you much in a jungle— and all that accurate clinical terminology doesn't translate very well to corporate America. That's because people at work have work to do and don't have time for psychological mumbo jumbo. It's simply the wrong tool for the job.

Functioning companies are intelligent, responsive, complex living systems. To superimpose a paradigm that evolved out of personal, psychological clinical work onto the richness of the minute-to-minute challenges and choices that face a growing corporate entity is absurd. The concepts of an outside expert—especially a clinically trained one—are going to have very little impact on that environment.

The Special Bonus of Therapy: We Know How to Control Ourselves

Therapists are particularly well suited to an egalitarian approach because of our training in self-management. The intensive interpersonal training we've gone through also serves to make us outstanding empowerment coaches. We've already learned how to moderate our responses in the service of the client's needs. Other coaches-in-training also have to struggle with self-identification as a helper and the habit of giving advice, but few of them have gone through the deep, insight-oriented inner work required of a psychotherapist. Thanks to our training as therapists, when we realize the negative impact controlling behavior can have on a client, we can modify our responses to better coach our clients. Once therapists stop trying to sneak therapy into coaching, therapists become outstanding empowerment coaches—primarily because of our self-awareness and our self-management abilities.

GIVING UP AUTHORITY

However, just reading a few paragraphs about authority may not be enough to persuade you to give up years of feeling in charge. So let's see exactly what's at stake here:

What do I enjoy the most about feeling competent and in control as a therapist? _____

_____

_____

_____

_____

_____

_____

_____

Where else in my life do I think I need to be the one in charge? _____

_____

_____

_____

_____

_____

_____

What might I get from letting go of my authority role when I coach? _____

_____

_____

_____

_____

_____

_____

_____

Now that you understand how different coaching is from therapy—and why it should be—here's an exercise to help you fully step into this new perspective:

A NEW PAIR OF GLASSES: WORKING WITH MENTALLY HEALTHY CLIENTS

(You can do this exercise in your imagination, but I recommend that you actually go to a drugstore and buy a pair of rose-tinted sunglasses and use them for a day.)

Imagine you have a pair of magical eyeglasses. When you put them on, you see everything and everyone as whole, perfect, radiant, and healthy exactly as they are. If they're in pain, it's a pain that teaches them important and necessary lessons, lessons they could learn no other way. If they're dissatisfied, it's a dissatisfaction that will eventually lead to growth. With these glasses on, you see nothing that you need to fix, help, correct, or make better.

Now imagine looking into a mirror. With the glasses on you see that you, too, are whole, perfect, radiant, and healthy exactly as you are. Nothing to change or improve. Exactly where you need to be.

These are the glasses you wear as a coach who empowers clients.

So let's get back to the question that opened this chapter: what is coaching? In a nutshell, coaching is a profession that assists mentally healthy people to achieve their personal and career goals.

CHAPTER FIVE

UNLEARNING WHAT WE KNOW

My first coaching supervisor was the late Laura Whitworth, one of the founders of the Coaches Training Institute. After listening to a half-hour taped session of my coaching, she said, "Well, David, that was a very nice therapy session, but it didn't have much to do with coaching."

That was when I realized that many of the great tricks I'd learned in twenty years of practicing psychotherapy would have to be unlearned just to become a beginner at this new enterprise. From both my own personal experience as a therapist-turned-coach, and my experience as a trainer and supervisor of coaches, I've identified nine key behaviors that therapeutically trained coaches typically have to unlearn in order to achieve excellence in the coaching profession. The following are nine common therapy practices *not* to transfer to coaching:

DON'T BEGIN A SESSION BY CHECKING IN WITH THE CLIENT

Although therapy is a focused activity, it's nowhere near as focused as coaching is. As therapists, we're inclined to begin a session by taking the emotional temperature of the client first, with a "How are you today?"

Coaches often start with "What's on your agenda for today's call?" Inherent in the difference between these two approaches is a difference in the motivation behind the interaction. Therapists are creating an environment in which a client will feel safe to share intimate details and insights, and thus start gently. Coaches, on the other hand, are creating a bold and empowering space in which a client can dream and risk. Coaches don't need to worry about the strength and quality of the connection between them and clients, because coaches know that their clients can take care of themselves; thus, coaches can get right to the work at hand.

CASE EXAMPLE: THERAPY VS. COACHING: STARTING THE SESSION

Therapy scenario: Client walks in, shoulders hunched over, brows furrowed, and dejectedly sits down.

Therapist: "You look like there's a lot going on today, Carl. What is it?"

Client: "I'm really discouraged."

Coaching scenario: Client calls in five minutes late.

Coach: "Hi, Carl."

Client: "Hi. Sorry I'm late. Nothing is going well today."

Coach: "Bummer. Sorry to hear that. Do you want to focus our coaching on that, or do you have another agenda for today's call?"

DON'T LOOK FOR PROBLEMS TO SOLVE

People don't go to therapy unless they have some sort of dysfunctional element in their life. Therapists excel at identifying problems and articulating them in a way that helps clients begin to solve them. This is a big part of how we make our living as psychotherapists.

A coach is much less interested in looking at problems. Problems are minor impediments in the path of achieving goals. Although any problem that really blocks this path needs to be addressed, the philosophy of coaching holds that the more time that's spent examining problems, the more problems the client will create. Better to focus on achievements—and have more of *them* to examine.

CASE EXAMPLE: THERAPY VS. COACHING: PROBLEMS

Scenario: Client is in the middle of a session.

Therapy:

Client: "Another thing I want to work on is my messed-up relationship with food."

Therapist: "What is your relationship with food?"

Coaching:

Client: "Another thing I want to work on is my messed-up relationship with food."

Coach: "Sounds like your Gremlin wants to use that to beat you up. Let's get her off the line and then see if there's anything left to coach about your relationship with food."

DON'T TALK ABOUT THE PAST

For the therapist, we are all products of our histories. Whether it's a neurotic pattern, a narrative script, or a false belief, our actions are structured by the events which have preceded a dysfunctional behavior, them. A coach is singularly uninterested in the past. What's done is done. The more important question is "What's in front of you?" This is why therapists sometimes characterize coaching as superficial cheerleading and coaches sometimes characterize therapy as self-indulgent navel-gazing.

CASE EXAMPLE: THERAPY VS. COACHING: THE PAST

Scenario: Client is talking about her agenda.

Therapy:

Client: "I never seem to have enough."

Therapist: "Is this a recurring pattern in your life?"

Coaching:

Client: "I never seem to have enough."

Coach: "Tell me what your life would be like with *more* than enough of everything."

DON'T LOOK FOR CAUSAL FACTORS

Why do people do what they do? This is usually one of the central questions that leads us to become therapists in the first place. We love uncovering causative factors, be they early childhood trauma, nonproductive behavioral patterns, maladaptive beliefs, or unconstructive systems of communication. Discovering the why of things is the first step in remediation.

A coach feels completely comfortable telling clients, "I don't really need to know why you're doing a particular thing. All I want to know is what you're going to do to change it." Coaches value new behavior over insight; adopting a new perspective on a situation is appreciated more than gaining a deeper understanding of it. After all, a deeper understanding of the box you're in doesn't change your presence in the box. A new perspective, however, can catapult you right out of the box and into a whole new way of being.

CASE EXAMPLE: THERAPY VS. COACHING: CAUSAL FACTORS

Scenario: A client who has invested much energy into creating his department is dissatisfied with some aspects of his job.

Therapy:

Client:	"My boss might get transferred, so I'm thinking about applying to other companies. I like most of my job here but I feel stuck. But I really like this company."
Therapist:	"Tell me more about what stuck feels like."

Coaching:

Client:	"My boss might get transferred, so I'm thinking about applying to other companies. I like most of my job here but I feel stuck. But I really like this company."
Coach:	"Imagine it's your company—the whole kit and caboodle is now yours. You own it. You may not have stock control, but you have the guiding vision and passion. How does owning the company change your perspective?"

DON'T GATHER DATA

Therapists weave together rich sources of data into a coherent pattern. This data includes direct observation, gathering historical information, and gleaning information about the current life of the client. Out of this body of information a theoretical therapeutic hypothesis is created and a treatment plan is designed and implemented. All the training that goes into becoming a clinician gives us a strong bias toward the gathering of information. Clients—grateful for a receptive ear—like to share information, and we like to receive it, knowing it will help us refine our schemata of our clients and their worlds.

Coaches who choose the egalitarian/empowering coaching path don't need much data. In fact, time spent listening to a data download can interfere with the business at hand. Coaches don't theorize, analyze, clarify, prescribe, or advise. Coaches trust that clients already know everything they need to know about a particular situation and don't need to waste time telling the coach about it. In fact, a coach might interrupt a client in the middle of a long story about a situation and say, "I don't need to know the particulars about it. Just tell me what you want and how you're going to get it."

CASE EXAMPLE: THERAPY VS. COACHING: GATHERING DATA

Scenario: Client is exploring her desire to go to Africa.

Therapy:

Client: "I can remember dreaming about going on safari as a kid. It's always been a dream of mine. When I was twelve..." (A long story about how the client's daydreams got her through difficult times.)

Therapist: "Um-hmm."

Coaching:

Client: "I can remember dreaming about going on safari as a kid. It's always been a dream of mine. When I was twelve—"

Coach: *(interrupting)* "I get how important this is for you. What's the plan for getting over there this year?"

DON'T EXPLORE FEELINGS

The affect—and the emotional substrata that underlies affect—is of direct concern to the therapist. Often, emotional content can interfere with effective communication. As therapists, much of our work is to unravel these highly charged strands. However, harnessing emotions into the service of a client tends to require a lot of digging and uncovering, room for client discharge, and a milieu that allows and supports the often primitive expression of feelings. Helping a client express appropriate affect and experience emotional responses that are adaptive and effective are integral goals in almost any form of therapy.

Coaching doesn't ignore the emotional realm. In coaching, feelings are regarded as a valuable part of the human experience, as well as valuable signposts to underlying values and goals—but feelings aren't mined in coaching the way they are in therapy. If feelings can lead to action, then they can serve the coaching. If a client begins a call with a lot of emotion, a brief time can be allotted to clear these feelings before getting to work. However, a coaching session spent just expressing feelings would be a coaching session wasted.

CASE EXAMPLE: THERAPY VS. COACHING: EXPLORING FEELINGS

Scenario: Client is very upset.

Therapy:

Client:　　　"And I just don't think I can stand another minute of it with him."

Therapist:　　"How does what he did make you feel?"

Coaching:

Client:　　　"And I just don't think I can stand another minute of it with him."

Coach:　　　"So what are you going to do?"

DON'T REASSURE CLIENTS THAT THEY'RE BEING HEARD

One of the things Laura Whitworth pointed out to me during my first coaching supervision was the number of times I said things like "yes," and "yeah," and "um-hmm." She made me look at how often I put my clients at ease and let them know—sometimes almost subliminally—that I was listening and valuing what they had to say. As therapists, we may do this almost unconsciously to make the therapy space safe and comfortable. By making these little noises we continually reassure clients that we are listening and that we really care about them.

However, these frequent offers of reassurance actually interfere with coaching. Remember, as the International Coach Federation states on its website, "every client is creative, resourceful, and whole"; coaching clients already know we're listening attentively to them. Coaching clients aren't insecure and don't need our constant reassurance in that regard. Furthermore, as Whitworth explained to me, these nice noises can actually take power away from times when we choose to speak. When a coach speaks, it isn't to comfort clients—it's to call clients into their power and greatness. Thus, awkward pauses, clunky moments, and dead silences can actually support powerful coaching. Remember: coaching clients don't expect you to make them feel nice and comfortable—they expect you to rock their world.

CASE EXAMPLE: THERAPY VS. COACHING: REASSURING NOISES

Scenario: Client is talking about a relationship issue.

Therapy:

Client:　　　"I didn't know what to do next."

Therapist:	"Um-hmm."
Client:	"So I just called her up."
Therapist:	"Yes."
Client:	"And that's when she told me it was off."

Coaching:

Client:	"I didn't know what to do next."

Coach is quiet, waiting.

Client:	"So I just called her up."

Coach waits silently, knowing the client is about to get to the point.

Client:	"And that's when she told me it was off."
Coach:	"So what do you know now?"

DON'T CREATE WORTH THROUGH SHARING INSIGHT

Clients willingly pay for a therapist's insight. They need someone "outside the box" to see their situation from a new angle. For therapy clients it's a relief to begin to understand their circumstances and not feel trapped by them.

Coaches, however, are paid to ask open-ended questions that inspire clients to their own insights—and I don't mean those sneaky, leading questions that lead clients to insights you've already had about their situation. No, I mean really open-ended questions, questions where the questioner wonders, "Wow, how will my client answer that?"

CASE EXAMPLE: THERAPY VS. COACHING: INSIGHT

Scenario: Client has just finished articulating a conflict at work.

Therapy:

Therapist:	"It sounds like those caretaking patterns we've found in your intimate relationships may also appear with figures of authority in your workplace. What do you think?"

Coaching:

Coach:	"What kind of relationship would you like to have with your supervisor?"

DON'T CREATE CLOSURE

Therapists are sensitive to the idea of psychotherapy as open-heart surgery in fifty-minute segments. We try to do what we can to close up any psychological material that may have erupted during a session, so the client can function in the outside world.

Coaches say, "Let them bleed." Because, as coaches, we trust that our clients are healthy, we don't have to worry about patching them up. Instead, we can give homework like, "I know you're feeling pretty raw right now at what you've explored today. See if you can stay as raw and open as you possibly can for the next week."

CASE EXAMPLE: THERAPY VS. COACHING: CLOSURE

Scenario: The end of a powerful session.

Therapy:

Therapist: "You've been through a lot in this session. I know you have to go back to work right after this session, but please spend a few moments in your car first, just breathing and feeling your body. Be extra careful and aware of traffic on your way back to the office—and hold yourself very gently throughout the next week. If you need to schedule an extra session toward the end of the week please give my answering service a call and I'll see what I can do."

Coaching:

Coach: "You've just ripped open a big can of worms. For the next week I want you to keep that can open. Feel the rawness and hurt as deeply as you can, and come back to next week's call with three stories of how it was living your life that vulnerable. Will you do that?"

COACHING: A WHOLE NEW WORLD

In the fourth edition of the *Alcoholics Anonymous—Big Book* (2002), right after the twelve steps comes the following paragraph:

> Many of us exclaimed, "What an order! I can't go through with it." Do not be discouraged. No one among us has been able to maintain anything like perfect adherence to these principles. We are not saints. The point is that we are willing to grow along spiritual lines. The principles we have set down are guides to progress. We claim spiritual progress rather than spiritual perfection. (p. 118)

While the points I've made here about coaching certainly aren't the twelve steps, I can imagine many therapists out there reading them and thinking, "What an order! Take away these skills and what do I have left?" The point is that coaching is a very different enterprise from therapy—many orders of magnitude different. Don't imagine coaching as therapy with a twist. It's a whole new world!

THERAPY VS. COACHING

Scenario: The client, a thirty-four-year-old account executive at a large advertising agency, opens his session with:

> "This week sucked. That account I talked about last week didn't sign with us. And since my manager is on vacation, I got stuck taking the flack from some friggin' VP when the deal fell apart. And my mom's sick again. I don't even want to go home after work, so the last three nights I've gone out and had a few drinks with some guys at the office, which is pissing Sara off. Plus, she hates the new apartment. And I haven't slept worth shit. So that's my week—how's yours?"

First, write down how you might respond to this scenario:

A typical therapeutic response:

> "It sounds like you've had a difficult week. Which of the things you've talked about stands out as a good place for us to start?"

This response establishes rapport, lets the client know he has been listened to, and begins to focus the session on the most pressing problem.

A typical coaching response:

> "My week was a lot better than yours. What do you want to do? We can take two minutes to clear out the yucky feelings left over from The Week That Sucked, or we can jump right into the agenda you want to work on today. What's your choice?"

The coach makes no assumptions about the state of the client, or what the client needs. Instead, the coach puts the responsibility for the session directly on the shoulders of the client. In this particular example the client replied, "I don't want to talk about any of that junk. I want to talk about the book I'm writing."

CHAPTER SIX

WHAT A COACHING SESSION SOUNDS LIKE

In this chapter we'll look at an abbreviated version of a typical coaching session. This will give you the opportunity both to observe good coaching and to see how the principles we've discussed actually get implemented.

First, a caveat: this is not earth-shattering coaching. Most coaching isn't—most coaching is matter-of-fact, even a little mundane. As with therapy, occasionally a coaching session will come along that changes a client's life forever. But most of coaching—like most of therapy—is much less dramatic. The following is an account of an actual coaching session (details have been changed to preserve the client's anonymity):

A TYPICAL COACHING SESSION

The client, Gary, is a real-estate salesman, who came to coaching at the suggestion of his broker. His first four years in the office, Gary was a top-producing agent, but then he hit a two-year slump. Coaching began with a two-hour, face-to-face intake session to determine Gary's values and goals for coaching (see chapter 7 for more details about intake sessions). Coaching continued in half-hour phone calls, three times a month. The following session took place three months into the coaching.

At the beginning of his career, Gary would spend three hours every morning making client calls. The first to arrive at the office, Gary would knock off fifty to seventy calls to prospective clients every morning, Monday through Friday. He did this all four years he was successful—and then hoped that by maintaining the leads he'd developed over the four years he could keep his production at this high level. But this strategy didn't work.

In his personal life, Gary's decision to change his routine was catalyzed by the birth of his son. He loved fatherhood and wanted to devote more time to his son rather than his workaholic schedule. He realized, too, that he needed to pay more attention to his wife instead of just working hard and thinking that breadwinning was all he needed to give her as a husband. He also wanted to lose weight and get back into mountain biking, an activity he loved but which he'd abandoned after entering real estate. For the past three sessions he'd been working on a marketing plan for the year.

Gary: "Hi, Coach. How're you doing?"

Coach: "Great. So, what's on the agenda for today's call?"

Gary: "Boy, right down to business, huh?"

Coach: "Yep. What's on your list?"

> *Notice that no time is spent on idle chatter. The client is paying for coaching, not a pleasant conversation.*

Gary: "Okay, so this marketing plan thing. You know, I'm thinking it's just so much bullshit— I'm not doing what I need to do to get clients, so what's the good of planning how much money I want to earn by December? I should just spend my time making calls, not dreaming about something that isn't happening."

> *So far there isn't a clear agenda for the call, just some pent-up frustration. It's important that the coach doesn't become attached to an idea like "making a marketing plan is essential to success." The coach must stay with the client's reality, not steer it in the direction the coach thinks the client should go.*

Coach: "You're thinking this planning might be a waste of time."

Gary: "Right."

Coach: "So what wouldn't be a waste of time?"

Gary: "Cold-calling."

Coach: "Which you told me last week that you hate now."

Gary: "Yeah."

Coach: "So I'm not clear here—I'm a little slow today, help me out. What do you want to focus on in today's call?"

> *A good coach is a stupid coach. Instead of trying to guess what Gary needs—or where he wants to go—the coach just asks him.*

Gary: "Okay. So instead of talking about my marketing plan for months from now, I want to focus on getting more clients now."

Coach: "Excellent. That's something I can understand. So today's agenda is how to get your next client ASAP, right?"

Gary: "Sure, that would be great."

Now the coach knows from previous sessions that this is an essential agenda for this client. The coach also knows that the client has not followed through on previous homework to make a certain number of calls every week. The coach decides that the client may be stuck in one approach or perspective on how to succeed. This is a tricky place—if the coach slips into consultant mode the coach may start to suggest all sorts of things the client could do. Although this may be useful coaching for this particular moment, ultimately it subtly undermines the coach-client relationship, encouraging the client to go to the coach for answers, rather than find them inside himself. The coach will then become the expert and the client infantilized. Instead, the coach decides to help the client find his own solution.

Coach: "Let's look at some ways you can achieve that goal. The situation you are in is 'How do I get my next client?'—right?"

Gary: "Right."

Coach: "And one way is spending hours cold-calling every morning, like you used to do, right?"

Gary: "Yes."

Coach: "What happens inside when you think about going to work tomorrow at seven and prospecting?"

Gary: "My stomach gets all tight and I feel like I want to puke."

Coach: "Good, so we'll call this the phone-and-puke strategy."

Gary laughs.

Coach: "So, what's another way to get a new client?"

Gary: "An old client could call me with a referral?"

Coach: "Oh, that's good—you're sitting at your desk and the phone rings and it's an old client with a referral. How does that feel?"

Gary: "I like it. I'm happy. It's a stroke of good luck."

Coach: "Right. Let's call that the drop-out-of-the-sky strategy."

Gary: "Perfect!"

Coach: "How else can you get a new client?"

Gary: "I don't know."

Gary is getting stuck now—time for some brainstorming. But again, the coach has to make sure brainstorming isn't just a sneaky way of throwing in an opinion about what Gary should do.

Coach: "I've got an idea!"

Gary: "Good."

Coach: "How about grabbing someone at random off the street and tying them to a chair and telling them they can't get up until they sign a contract?"

Gary: "I like it!"

Coach: "How is it to be in front of your bound victim—oops, I mean, potential client?"

Gary: *(laughing)* "Well, I feel a little more powerful than I do facing the damn telephone."

Coach: "Good. We'll call it the kidnapping strategy. Now what's another way?"

Gary: "Well, it definitely felt good to be face-to-face with a client."

Coach: "Hmm, cool. Okay, how could you get face-to-face without kidnapping?"

Gary: "Well, you know, I've handed off my open house showings to other agents, but maybe I could start doing some myself."

Coach: "Okay, you're at an open house and a potential buyer comes in. How does it feel to be talking to her?"

Gary: "Hey, that feels great. I know how to work them, and it's not such a grind as making cold calls."

This is more alive than Gary has sounded since he started the call. But it's important to always open up more possibilities, not just decide what the client should choose.

Coach: "Okay, so we have four strategies now for how you can get your next client: phone-and-puke, drop-out-of-the-sky, kidnapping, and open houses. We need one more. What is it?"

Gary: "Well, there's a lender that comes through our office. Last week he was talking about doing a home buyers seminar. I could team up with him and we could do that together."

Coach: "Very cool. The seminar strategy. Do we want one more?"

Gary: "I don't think so."

As always, it's important to ground coaching in specific, actionable homework.

Coach: "So, these all sound like good ideas—although the kidnapping one may have a few legal problems attached to it. I want you to choose one that you will implement, without fail, this next week."

Gary: "Well, I have an open house scheduled at my listing on Kenilworth this Sunday. I got Francine to cover it for me, but I could take it back—or better yet, we could both do it. I think plenty of folks will come to see this place."

Coach: "Okay, so here's your homework: do the open house this weekend and come back with a new client for our call next week."

Gary: *(laughing)* "Absolutely!"

Coach: "This was a great job—in only twelve minutes you moved from feeling stuck to designing a plan of action that you're excited about. I love how you played with the kidnapping idea and turned it into doing open houses. That was really creative."

Gary: "Yeah, it was pretty cool, wasn't it?"

Coach: "Okay, so we have fifteen minutes left on this call. What else is on your agenda?"

CHANGING A POINT OF VIEW

In the excerpt we just read, the coach used a specific tool to broaden the viewpoint of the client: changing a point of view.

COACHING SKILL: Changing a Point of View

Goal: Sometimes clients get stuck in a limited perspective of what their options are. They imagine they have either no choices or just very limited options. The goal of this tool is both to open up a limited point of view and have the client commit to taking action from this new worldview.

Tool: Take a client through a specific series of eight steps (following) to arrive at a choice not previously imagined possible.

Using the previous example, here are the eight steps to changing a point of view:

Step 1: Name the Situation

In working to change a client's point of view, it's easy to end up sidetracked, having lost focus on the point of the exercise. By naming the situation—and repeatedly returning to this name—both client and coach stay on track. The name of the situation in the preceding example was "How can I get my next client?" The coach repeatedly framed questions using that phrase, to remind the client of the focus of the exercise.

Step 2: Briefly Flesh Out Known Options

Next, the coach wants to sketch out any viewpoints the client is already familiar with. This isn't a data-gathering mission—the client already knows these options very well, and the coach doesn't need more information about them to proceed. The focus here is on getting the client to feel what it's like to use these strategies. The question the coach used in the preceding example to do this was "What happens inside when you think about going to work tomorrow at seven and prospecting?"

Step 3: Name Each Option

Have fun with this, especially with options that seem painful and onerous to the client. Naming cold-calling "the phone-and-puke strategy" gave the client the freedom to laugh at it, not just feel enslaved by it. By naming each option after the client has expressed what it would feel like to use the option, the coach creates a language out of the client's own words that will set up later choice-making steps.

Step 4: Bring in New Points of View

The best person to do this is the client. Keep encouraging the client to imagine other ways of coping with the situation. As a coach, you'll have to carefully manage yourself at this point. It's tempting in this step—and the next—to throw in your own ideas. However, although you get a little narcissistic thrill at being the expert every time you do this, you do it at the expense of your client's empowerment. Don't do it!

Step 5: Brainstorming

Sometimes this step can be skipped. When a client comes up with three or four fresh perspectives you may not need to brainstorm. But if the client seems stuck, you can throw in some perspectives of your own to jump-start the creative process. The only reason to brainstorm is to help clients look outside the box they've created. Disguising opinions as zany ideas is cheating; trust the client's genius—stop trying to help! Offbeat and funny alternatives work best for this step.

Step 6: Ask for One More

Often you'll sense a click when a client lands on an exciting new way to see a situation. At this point, the temptation is to jump into commitment—resist this urge and fish just a little more. In the preceding example, the click happened at the idea of doing open houses. However, in the next session Gary returned to the idea of conducting seminars—which ultimately proved highly successful for him. He developed a seminar called "Forget Stocks, Retire with Real Estate" and soon exceeded his previous sales record.

Step 7: Choice and Action

A client with good ideas is a client who's still stuck. Good ideas are like airplanes in a holding pattern, endlessly circling the airport. Remember, the goal of this exercise is two-pronged: both to open up a client's limited point of view and to have the client commit to taking action from this new worldview. Step seven is the take-action step. Ask the client to choose a point of view and design a specific, measurable, actionable piece of homework from this new point of view to implement the following week. This will land a plane—now a good idea is translated into action. In the preceding example the coach said, "I want you to choose one that you will implement, without fail, this next week." The coach then repeated the action Gary chose—doing an open house—so that the homework assignment was crystal clear to both client and coach.

Step 8: Acknowledgment

Clients work hard in this process. Acknowledging who a client had to be in order to be successful in changing a point of view can be a nice way to close the experience.

Try this technique out on a volunteer coaching client. You can use the following worksheet to keep notes on what the client said, to remind yourself of the steps, and to document what homework the client committed to.

CHANGING A POINT OF VIEW

Client's name: _____ Date: _____

Step 1: Name the situation

Step 2: Briefly flesh out known options

Step 3: Name each option

Step 4: Bring in new points of view

Step 5: Brainstorming

Step 6: Ask for one more

Step 7: Choice and action

Step 8: Acknowledgment

CHAPTER SEVEN

WHAT AN INTAKE SESSION SOUNDS LIKE

Once a client has chosen you as her coach, a longer than normal *intake session* is scheduled for you and the client to design your working relationship. What constitutes longer than normal? I know one coach who lives with new clients for a week or so. More commonly, however, intake sessions are one-and-a-half to two hours long.

Unlike with regular coaching, I prefer to do intake sessions face-to-face if possible—and preferably on the client's turf, at his home or office. This gives me insights into the client's world that I might not have accumulated had I done the intake via the phone. Meeting each other in person also makes the relationship more personal and intimate. But meeting in person is certainly not a prerequisite; I have many clients whom I have never met.

Every intake session has a life of its own, but there are three basic topics that need to be covered, usually in the following order:

1. What does the client think and feel about all aspects of her current life?

2. What inspires and motivates the client?

3. What is the specific nature of the work that the coach and client will be involved in?

This chapter will take you through the intake process and introduce three essential tools: the satisfaction matrix, the passions list, and the fundamental objectives list, all of which will be useful in your intake sessions.

TURNING DOWN THE VOLUME OF GREMLINS

Often I begin intake sessions—but only intake sessions, not regular coaching sessions—with a very short check-in to help clients clear away any life-static from the day, so that they can be truly present for the coaching process. After that's accomplished, I'll introduce the concept of the Gremlin. I'll explain, "The Gremlin is the doubting voice inside your head that's always carping, always telling you that you're not doing things well enough, or that you should be doing something else." To turn down the volume of the Gremlin we then personify it.

Clients need to see the Gremlin as something clearly different from themselves: a voice in their heads—but not a trustworthy one. By giving Gremlins names and faces we facilitate this process.

COACHING SKILL: Personifying the Gremlin

Goal: To create an image that embodies the voice of inner judgment and belittlement, in the service of limiting its power.

Tool: Use simple imagery to depict the Gremlin as something distinct from the psyche of the client.

To personify a Gremlin, follow the three-step process outlined below.

Step 1: Collect Gremlin Verbiage

Let the Gremlin expose itself—listen to the ridiculous injunctions it spouts. Ask, "What are some of the things your Gremlin, your inner judge, says about you?" By laughing together over some of the more ridiculous things the Gremlin says, you build an alliance between client and coach and against the Gremlin.

Step 2: Paint a Face on It

Ask, "If you had to paint me a picture of your Gremlin, what would it look like?" If the client blocks on this, suggest instead, "What cartoon character does your Gremlin remind you of?" The focus here is on finding a ridiculous image, not a terrifying one. Once accomplished, ask the client to give this critter a name.

Step 3: Create a Gremlin-Free Space for the Intake Session

Ask the client what he needs to do to get the Gremlin out of the room so you two can have a great intake session. (See chapter 3 for more Gremlin management tools.)

Of course, it always pays to apply these techniques to yourself first:

PERSONIFYING YOUR GREMLIN

1. Name your Gremlin: _____

2. What kind of junk does your Gremlin typically say to you?

3. Draw a sketch of it below:

THE SATISFACTION MATRIX

To get a complete picture of the lives of our clients, we use the *satisfaction matrix*. The satisfaction matrix is a tool for taking snapshots of clients' levels of satisfaction and fulfillment across the spectrum of their life.

COACHING SKILL: The Satisfaction Matrix

Goal: To create a visual representation of how clients self-evaluate their life in terms of the satisfaction and fulfillment it gives them.

Tool: Use the Satisfaction Matrix to graphically chart levels of satisfaction.

Four Steps for Using the Matrix

To use the satisfaction matrix with clients, follow these four steps:

STEP 1: INTRODUCTION

I usually introduce the satisfaction matrix by saying something like, "I'd like to capture a snapshot of how satisfied and fulfilled you feel right now in certain aspects of your life. This isn't about how your life was, or how you want it to be. It's about your life today."

STEP 2: FILLING OUT THE FORM

Next, the client fills out the matrix. To help a client do so, I might say something like, "Imagine each rectangular segment as a container. You want to fill it with a liquid that represents your level of satisfaction and fulfillment in that particular area of your life. If you feel completely dissatisfied in an area, you can leave it empty. If you feel completely fulfilled in an area, you can fill it all the way up to 100 percent. Or, pick the percentage between the two that represents your level of fulfillment today. Any questions?"

STEP 3: FLESHING OUT THE SECTIONS

The actual numbers the client chooses aren't the meat of this tool. Once the client has filled out the satisfaction matrix, the coach takes it back and goes through each section with the client. Use questions like:

THE SATISFACTION MATRIX

Name: _____ Date: _____

Shade in each category to the level you feel satisfied and fulfilled in this area today; then write down the number that shading represents. For example, if you feel pretty satisfied in the category of your current job, profession, or career—but not totally fulfilled—you might fill in that category to look like this:

EXAMPLE:

	Utter Dissatisfaction 0%	In the Middle 50%	Completely Fulfilled 100%
current job, profession, or career			(75%)

	Utter Dissatisfaction 0%	In the Middle 50%	Completely Fulfilled 100%
current job, profession, or career			
most intimate personal relationship			
family (however you define it)			
relationship with money and finances			
physical health, diet, and exercise program			
mental health and emotional well-being			
friends and community			
ongoing education; personal and spiritual growth			
hobbies, fun, travel, and enjoyment			

"Tell me more about what 60 percent satisfied in fun and recreation means to you."

"Where would you like this percentage to be?"

"What would 200 percent look like?" (If an area is already at 100 percent.)

"What is something you can do to increase this number?"

"Which of these sections seem most relevant to our coaching work?"

It's important not to make assumptions about these findings. A low percentage in some areas may be just fine for the client. A client may be more interested in raising a 90 percent in one area to 100 percent than in dealing with an area at 10 percent. It's not your job to choose what a client needs to work on. Accept clients at their word.

STEP 4: TAKE LOTS OF NOTES

The conversations that arise from the satisfaction matrix are rich. My notes on what a client has said about each of these sections are more valuable to me than any measurement. I end up scrawling all over this sheet; in particular, I star areas the client has identified as areas to focus on in our coaching.

The Satisfaction Matrix: Self-Survey

You cannot truly appreciate this tool until you've applied it to yourself. Use the following matrix and the questions listed above in step 3 to examine the levels of satisfaction and fulfillment in your own life, today. Afterwards, write a little about what you discovered about yourself.

PERSONIFYING PASSIONS

Coaches need to know what motivates clients. Each of us has a unique list of values, passions, standards, and beliefs that inspires us into action. These are the things that get us out of bed in the morning ready to take on the day. These are the things that make our lives meaningful and precious. These are why we do what we do.

Unfortunately, each of us also has an equally long list of rules, injunctions, judgments, and "shoulds" that mask themselves as values. While these superego commandments may push us into action, ultimately they act as barriers to fulfillment.

THE SATISFACTION MATRIX

Name: _____ Date: _____

Shade in each category to the level you feel satisfied and fulfilled in this area today; then write down the number that shading represents. For example, if you feel pretty satisfied in the category of your current job, profession, or career—but not totally fulfilled—you might fill in that category to look like this:

EXAMPLE:

	Utter Dissatisfaction 0%	In the Middle 50%	Completely Fulfilled 100%
current job, profession, or career			(75%)

	Utter Dissatisfaction 0%	In the Middle 50%	Completely Fulfilled 100%
current job, profession, or career			
most intimate personal relationship			
family (however you define it)			
relationship with money and finances			
physical health, diet, and exercise program			
mental health and emotional well-being			
friends and community			
ongoing education; personal and spiritual growth			
hobbies, fun, travel, and enjoyment			

COACHING SKILL: Personifying Passions

Goal: To connect clients with the fundamental passions that make their life meaningful and motivate constructive action.

Tool: Use a *passions list*—a list of the compelling, motivating elements of an individual client's psyche—to inspire a client to action, especially when the going gets rough.

To create a passions list, follow these four steps:

Step 1: Unearth Passions

The trick behind this exercise is to keep it from being exclusively mental. Direct your questioning toward a felt sense of these elements, not just an intellectual understanding of them. The following are some questions you can use to unearth these passions—ask one and then follow the client's answers to find the underlying value:

"What do you think are your core passions, values, and beliefs?"

"What are some things that inspire you?"

"What do you love?"

"What must you have in your life for it to be meaningful?"

"What do you enjoy?"

"Remember one of the worst times in your life; you don't have to tell me about it. What precious passion, value, or belief was being undermined or hurt in that circumstance?"

"Remember one of the best times in your life. Tell me about it—what precious passion, value, or belief was alive and present in that circumstance?"

"What would your intimate partner add to this list in terms of your core passions, values, and beliefs?"

Don't try to attach "correct" names to this experience. Some values clarification tools end up looking like checklists for boy scouts: "Check the ones that apply: trustworthy, loyal, helpful, friendly, courteous, kind, obedient, cheerful, thrifty, brave, clean, reverent." Instead, stay very close to the client's words for the experience. The following example shows how to use an unearthing question effectively, following it to discover the client's underlying passion.

CASE EXAMPLE: UNEARTHING QUESTIONS

Coach: "What do you love?"

Client: "I love my daughter Melissa."

Coach: "Tell me one thing about Melissa that you cherish."

Client: "There are so many things! Well, I love it when she runs up to me and throws her arms around me and lets me swing her up off the floor."

Coach: "And what do you feel in that moment?"

Client: "I am so happy. She is pure joy."

Coach: "So there's this swinging, hugging, joyous, happy feeling."

Client: "Yes."

Coach: "And it's one of the things that makes your life worth living."

Client: "Absolutely!"

Coach: "Let's call this the swinging-hugging-joyous-happiness value for now."

Step 2: Distill to Essence/Personify the Passion

In this next step we take the raw notes we've just unearthed and create a name we can use for this inspirational passion/value/belief. Again the name needs to come from the client; it's best when the name refers to an image, person, or clear symbol, rather than a concept.

In the previous example the coach could have said, "Let's call this aliveness." But this is actually much less alive than "swinging-hugging-joyous-happiness." In this phase the coach might suggest, "Do you want to take this swinging-hugging-joyous-happiness value and call it Melissa-and-me, or is there a better name for it? Maybe we can just leave it at swinging-hugging-joyous-happiness. What do you think?"

The following example is from an intake session my coach did with me:

CASE EXAMPLE: PERSONIFYING THE PASSION

Client: "I need to have discipline with my writing if I want to succeed."

Coach: "Okay. First, let's make sure the Gremlin hasn't just snuck in here with a commandment: *thou must write!*"

Client: "Oh, no. I get the difference. The voice that tells me I'm a bad person for not writing, that's the Gremlin. This is something different. It's like a grown-up voice that says, 'Okay, stop your whining, and go over there and get to work.' It's tough—like the Gremlin—but it really wants me to succeed, not just feel rotten about myself."

Coach: "Whose voice does it sound like?"

Client: "Well, kind of like my dad's—but then, my Gremlin sounds like my dad, too, so I don't want any part of that."

Coach: "Is there a writer whose voice sounds like it?"

Client: *(laughing)* "Yeah. Norman Mailer. It's a prizefighter-tough-guy-Norman-Mailer voice that says, 'Look, buddy, all the excuses in the world ain't gonna write no novel. Now go to your desk and don't get up until you got twenty pages of manuscript.'"

Coach: "Perfect. Shall we call the voice Norman Mailer?"

Client: "Right on!"

Step 3: Prioritize

Often, the two preceding steps will generate dozens of passions and values. Now it's time to get to the central, core ones. On a separate piece of paper, make a list of the many passions and values that have surfaced in talking with your client. You'll immediately see one of the advantages of personifying these elements: creating this list becomes simple. Hand this list to your client and say something like, "Okay, you don't have to rank these—just put a check mark next to the five core passions in your life." If a client has trouble with this, I'll sometimes say, "You can bunch some of them together if you think they might be the same thing," or "In your case I'll make a special exception and let you have six core values."

After the client has grumbled but accomplished the task, you can say, "Okay, now take those five core passions and rank them in terms of priority. I know all of them are important to you, but which has the most importance to who you are—in the world and in your heart?"

Step 4: Assess Embodiment

Next it's time to assess how fully the client is currently embodying these core values. First, write the client's five core passions on a separate page. Hand this page to the client and say, "We're going to look at how fully you embody each of these. Please invite your Gremlin to leave the room. This isn't about judgment. No one embodies all their passions and values every minute of the day, so relax. Next to each one of these give yourself a score from 1 to 10. A 1 means 'Oh yeah, that's important, and I really have to get around to doing that someday.' A 5 means 'In some way during half of my waking hours I am living this value and honoring this passion.' A 10 means 'With every waking breath I live this fully.'"

When the client has completed this, ask her what she notices about her core passions and values and how she lives them.

Use the following worksheet in your intake sessions to guide you through this process:

THE PASSIONS LIST

Client's Name: _____ Date: _____

Step 1: Unearth Passions

"What do you think are your core passions, values, and beliefs?"

"What are some things that inspire you?"

"What do you love?"

"What must you have in your life for it to be meaningful?"

"What do you enjoy?"

"Remember one of the worst times in your life; you don't have to tell me about it. What precious passion, value, or belief was being undermined or hurt in that circumstance?"

"Remember one of the best times in your life. Tell me about it—what precious passion, value, or belief was alive and present in that circumstance?"

"What would your intimate partner add to this list in terms of your core passions, values, and beliefs?"

Step 2: Distill to Essence/Personify the Passion

FIRST PASSION:

Words:

Image:

Name:

SECOND PASSION:

Words:

Image:

Name:

THIRD PASSION:

Words:

Image:

Name:

FOURTH PASSION:

Words:

Image:

Name:

FIFTH PASSION:

Words:

Image:

Name:

SIXTH PASSION:

Words:

Image:

Name:

SEVENTH PASSION:

Words:

Image:

Name:

EIGHTH PASSION:

Words:

Image:

Name:

NINTH PASSION:

Words:

Image:

Name:

TENTH PASSION:

Words:

Image:

Name:

Step 3: Prioritize

Mark the five core passions of your life. Order them from 1 to 5, based on how important they are to your life, with 1 being the most important and 5 being the least important.

1.

2.

3.

4.

5.

Step 4: Assess Embodiment

Using a scale of 1 to 10, express how you embody each of those five passions in your everyday life. Remember, a 1 means "Oh yeah, that's important, and I really have to get around to doing that someday"; a 5 means "In some way during half of my waking hours I am living this value and honoring this passion"; and a 10 means "With every waking breath I live this fully."

What do you notice about your core values and how you embody them?

FOCUSING THE COACHING

The intake session often concludes with the client and the coach defining the specific nature of the work they're coming together to do. The tool to accomplish this is very simple.

COACHING SKILL: Identifying the Fundamental Objectives of the Coaching

Goal: To determine the specific nature of the work the coaching will focus on.

Tool: Use the following three steps to create a fundamental objectives list.

Step 1: Review

Have the client review the satisfaction matrix and passions list he's already created. Often, upon rereading these, a client will find new passions that need to be included—or see some connections that weren't previously visible. Having these center stage will help the client see how coaching can serve both his passions and his whole life.

Step 2: Frame the Exercise

Introduce the plan to create a fundamental objectives list by saying something like, "Okay, now we have the context of your life as you're living it right now, and the core passions and values that you want to honor in your life. Now it's time to get specific about what you want us to focus on during our coaching. Let's identify five objectives to focus our coaching on."

Step 3: Get Clear Objectives

When establishing an objective, first make sure it's coachable. By this I mean that the objective is something the client herself can accomplish. An agenda like "get elected president" isn't coachable; others are required to accomplish this goal. However, "gain power in my political party, and position myself for a presidential nomination" is coachable. The more specific the goal the better. "Make a ton of money" isn't as good as "make at least $100,000 in the next twelve months."

Some clients will just dictate the areas they want coaching on; write these down and you're through. Other clients may need help in getting to clear, coachable objectives. Here are some places you can look for objectives:

✓ The areas in the client's satisfaction matrix that you starred because the client indicated he wanted to focus coaching on them.

✓ Discrepancies between the client's core values and their embodiment.

✓ The fun/play/leisure area and the health/diet/fitness area of the satisfaction matrix, two areas that often get neglected in our busy lives.

✓ Any intuition you may have about a target area.

Use the following worksheet to record the five objectives the client has identified:

THE FUNDAMENTAL OBJECTIVES OF OUR COACHING

Client: _____ Coach: _____ Date: _____

Objective 1:

Objective 2:

Objective 3:

Objective 4:

Objective 5:

It's important to self-manage your opinions out of this list. What *you* think your client should work on is irrelevant. If you trust that your clients are mentally healthy, then you can also trust what they want for their agendas. This isn't about unearthing psychodynamics or confronting resistance. Often there will be large parts of your clients' lives that they won't want coaching on. One client said to me, "My relationship with my family is at zero, and that's precisely where I want it to be." You have to be able to honor and trust that this is perfect for this client. Give up your notions about correct mental health and return to the real world of your client.

Once you have completed the fundamental objectives list, ask the client which of these objectives she would like to focus on in the time between the intake session and the next coaching session. Then create homework for this objective. Look for specific actions the client can take during this period to move some of these goals forward. Your intake session is now complete!

CHAPTER EIGHT

SAMPLE SESSIONS THAT SPARKLE

One of the major areas where coaching and psychotherapy differ is in how we obtain clients. Because of the nature of our work as psychotherapists, marketing our services is limited to presenting educational workshops, writing books, discreet advertising, and referrals. As a coach, almost any form of self-promotion you can conceive of is acceptable.

For coaches, the most common form of self-promotion is giving away a taste of our services. We call these *sample sessions*. Sample sessions are short coaching sessions, most often done on the telephone. Because of sample sessions, newcomers to the coaching field compete on a level playing field with even the most experienced coaches.

Clients looking for a coach will often shop around, trying sample sessions with a number of coaches before deciding on which coach they want to work with. Attracting clients is more about how clients feel about you as their coach than it is about comparing resumés. However, this can feel a bit like an audition, and can intimidate therapists-turned-coaches who aren't used to competing for clients.

This chapter will take some of the fear out of sample sessions. You'll learn how to structure sample sessions and how to make them successful.

THE FIVE STEPS TO SUCCESSFUL SAMPLE SESSIONS

To deliver a sparkling, successful sample session, you need to follow just five steps:

1. Set up the session.

2. Set the frame for the session; explain—briefly—and dive into coaching.

3. Coach dangerously.

4. Give homework that requires future contact.

5. Ask for the business.

Step 1: Set Up the Session

The first step in doing a sample session is to set it up in a way that serves you. When someone contacts you, thanks to your excellent marketing and promotion efforts (see chapters 11 and 12 for more information on marketing and promotion), you need to reply immediately. Calls (and e-mails) from prospective clients take precedence over calls from current clients, other business calls, or just about anything. They are your lifeblood for future business. Clients appreciate a rapid response, and by responding immediately you set yourself apart from your competitors.

I recommend you do this initial contact by phone, rather than e-mail. Prospective clients will bond more favorably with a voice than with an e-mail. In this initial call don't explain much about your process, unless the client absolutely demands information. The goal is to set up the sample session, not disqualify yourself due to some immaterial standard the client may have. What I usually say is "That's a great question, and unless you really need an answer right now, I'd love to talk about that with you after you get a taste of how I coach. When could we set up a half-hour call to do that?" Since the sample session is free, most clients are only too glad to accommodate you.

Unlike regular coaching, I will often set up the sample session so that I call the prospective client. That way I'm in control—not sitting around waiting for a call that may or may not come. A percentage of prospective clients will fail to show; I don't want to waste my time on them. Often I send an e-mail reminder the day before our session is scheduled. Folks are busy—it's easy for them to forget you at this stage in the process.

Step 2: Set the Frame for the Session

It's important to make the sample session useful, safe, and exciting for clients. Even more important is clearly offering your coaching services and asking clients to choose you as their coach. A frame fulfills all these functions. I keep mine pretty simple; at the start of a sample session I say something like, "I'm really looking forward to this call. I enjoy giving away a sample of my coaching. Here's how I'd like this call to go: I'd like to start out by coaching you for fifteen minutes or so. I'm going to coach you as though you're already my client. This isn't a simulation, it's the real thing. Afterwards, I'd love to answer any questions you may have. And then we'll see if we fit as coach and client. Does that work for you?"

By setting the frame you establish your professionalism and the structure of the call. And by beginning with actual coaching you circumvent a lot of unnecessary discussion about what coaching is and what specifically you do as a coach. Opening with coaching cuts the sales pitch and takes the client right out on a test drive.

The other thing the frame does is set you up to ask prospective clients for their business later. Prospective clients know this isn't just a nice chat or an information-gathering session. They will be asked to make a decision at the end of the call.

Step 3: Coach Dangerously

Years ago, I was the staffing coordinator for a treatment center serving schizophrenic adolescents. As part of their initial orientation, potential staff members would spend a few hours at our school. The school could be a wild place at times. I noticed that the potential staff members who were around during altercations—particularly those who accidentally got hit—nearly always chose to join up. People like danger—coaches and coaching clients included.

When you believe clients are naturally creative, resourceful, and whole, you have full permission to ask them anything. You don't have to worry about damaging fragile psyches because coaching clients aren't fragile. Coaching clients can take care of themselves—which includes not answering your questions if they don't want to. Coaching dangerously comes when the coach wonders, "What question would shake this client's world?"—and then asks it.

Therapists often struggle with the idea of coaching dangerously. This comes from previously working only with mentally ill people. As therapists, we're deeply concerned with making the therapeutic environment safe for our clients. Making clients feel safe is a major part of our job as therapists.

It's not in the job description of a coach. In fact, most coaching clients actually hunger for wise challenging that calls them to heights they never envisioned for themselves. In the sample session, the coach's job is to blow a prospective client away with the possibilities and potential the client already possesses—in only fifteen minutes and mostly through asking questions.

Quite a challenge for the coach! But we're setting the bar high for both client and coach in this sample session. Some prospective clients won't like it and will go away. Some people aren't ready for coaching—they'd prefer to narcissistically download and receive acknowledgment, without being asked to change. These clients aren't much fun to coach. Guess what? You don't have to coach them! If you feel you're doing all the work in the sample session and the prospective client is dragging his heels, at the end of the call say something like, "I don't think I'm a good coach for you. Let me give you the names of a couple of other coaches you might want to try." As coaches we don't have to take whoever comes through our door. Don't you love coaching?

CASE EXAMPLE: COACHING DANGEROUSLY

Scenario: The client comes into the sample session with the following agenda:

Client: "I just feel so stifled in this job. I know what I want to do, but right now I need the money. It just isn't the right time to quit, because we've got all these bills coming in. But I can feel the walls closing in on me. I need some help looking at this whole thing differently so I can make it through the next six months."

Safe coaching:

Coach: "So what kind of support do you need from the people around you to help you make it through this time?"

Dangerous coaching:

Coach: "So here's my challenge to you. Write your resignation letter, dating it six months from today, and put it in an envelope fully addressed to your boss. Next, send it to me—and know that I will mail it six months from today. As with any coaching challenge you can say yes or no or renegotiate. Do you accept my challenge?"

Step 4: Give Homework That Requires Future Contact

I need to underline a fact that might make you a little uncomfortable: the point of the sample session is to sell your services. As a therapist, you usually didn't need to compete for business. Therefore, from your very first contact with your client your focus was exclusively on what was best for her. In fact, most therapists are specifically trained to put their needs and desires second to the needs of the work. Some therapies call this managing countertransference. It means that your hard focus stays at all times on your client.

Welcome to the wonderful world of sales. It is *not* the job of a sample session to serve the client. Yes, the prospective client needs excellent coaching, but the sample session is for one purpose only: to move prospective clients to a choice point, where prospective clients either choose you as their coach or they don't.

As you coach, look for homework that will require the client to talk with you again. This can be quite easy.

CASE EXAMPLE: GIVING HOMEWORK THAT REQUIRES FUTURE CONTACT

Scenario: In a sample session, the prospective client realizes that he is giving his power away. He creates homework around saying no to people in his life.

Coach: "So, your homework is to say no at least three times a day for a week, and on every workday, at least one of those times must be at work."

Client: "Right!"

Coach: "So I just want to tweak it a little. Can I call you at this time next week and check in with you about the homework, and see how it went?"

Client: "Sure, that would be great!"

The neat thing about giving homework that requires future contact is that it accomplishes two things: One, it conveys to clients that you really do care about them and their homework. Two, it ensures another conversation in which you can ask the prospective client to be your client. Machiavellian? Not really. Just serving both you and your client. You get to do that as a coach—no more mandatory selfless service.

Step 5: Ask for the Business

This final step has derailed many a therapist looking to add coaching to their repertory. Although these prospective coaches may have created beautiful brochures, paid for advertising, conducted workshops, created referral systems, and done sample sessions, they leave out this final step, feeling that it makes them look like used-car salesmen. And they flounder as coaches. Some leave the profession resentful, some blame themselves—but without really understanding the problem.

Here's the situation in a nutshell: when you're dealing with mentally healthy people, you have to ask them to choose you to be their coach. We don't have to do that as therapists. Asking for business can seem scary and unappetizing. Get over it! The prospective coaching client is waiting for you to ask her to be your client. Prospective clients don't know whether you want them as clients. And prospective clients are often hesitant to make a choice—they'd prefer to keep shopping around, comparing, contrasting, procrastinating. They'll do exactly that until some coach asks them to choose. They will probably choose this coach. Let this coach be you.

Five words can spell the difference between a successful coach and a resentful, self-deprecating failure. Say the words to your prospective client at the end of a sample session and watch the miracle unfold. *Don't* say them and you and your prospective client will leave the session feeling unfinished. Ready? Here they are: "Will you be my client?"

Practice saying them aloud. Say them a hundred times, until the question flows naturally out of your mouth. This question may make the prospective client uncomfortable for a moment. So what? As a coach, lots of your questions are going to make clients uncomfortable. You are calling them forth to make a clear choice.

If the answer is no, don't stop yet—there is one more essential question that still needs to be asked. Usually, when we hear no, our narcissistic egos want to run in the opposite direction. We make nice noises and try to get away as soon as possible. But you're a coach now, and running away serves neither your prospective client nor the building of your practice. Really—hang in there for just one more question and you may end up getting a third of those no sayers as clients. Magic question number two is: "What exactly does that no mean?"

Prepare to be surprised. We tend to assume that a no is related to some deficiency we have as coaches. Actually, you'll often hear things like, "It means that I'm not quite ready to decide." Or, "I need to get the money together." Or an unspoken "Ask me again." I can't tell you how many prospective clients have initially said no and then gone on to become clients. Many have expressed relief that I didn't disappear when they said no. They appreciated my tenacity in sticking with them through their initial resistance. So before you give up on a prospective client, find out what that no really means.

SAMPLE SESSIONS: JUST DO IT

The next two minutes may very well determine your success as a coach. I'm going to give you a challenge. You can take the challenge on, or you can skip over it and continue reading. If you skip it and just keep reading, there's a very good chance that you'll spend several months getting ready to get ready—and may never end up becoming a coach. If you take it on right now, you'll demonstrate to yourself (the only person who matters) that you are truly serious about becoming a coach.

You can't learn things like coaching dangerously or asking for business unless you actually practice them in the real world. Unlike psychotherapy, you don't need a bunch of degrees and a nice office before you can begin coaching. But you do need real-world practice. You will not become a good coach unless you start coaching now.

So here is my challenge: Right now, call someone and set up a sample session. In that sample session, ask for the business. Go out and get your first coaching client today.

If you keep reading and put this off, you're betraying yourself. If you put the book down and pick up the phone, you're starting a magnificent adventure. Go forth and do great work!

CHAPTER NINE

COACHING YOURSELF

You wouldn't buy a car without taking it for a test drive. So, too, you wouldn't want to commit to being a coach until you've given the coaching profession a test drive. The best way to do this is to hire a coach, but you can also experiment with some self-coaching. Needless to say, anything you learn on yourself can be used later with clients. This chapter is one long experiential exercise in self-coaching. Here goes...

COACHABLE VS. UNCOACHABLE AGENDAS

In chapter 7 we introduced the idea of defining coachable agendas with your clients. A coachable agenda is a prerequisite to success for every coaching interaction. Without it, coaching may wander into psychotherapy or degenerate into conversation or just advice. When an agenda is clear, coaching stays crisp and focused.

COACHING SKILL: Establishing a Coachable Agenda

Goal: To frame a client's issue so that the client is ready to be coached on it.

Tool: Use the following Coachability Index to learn which agendas are coachable and which are not.

THE COACHABILITY INDEX

The Coachable Agenda

Score 10 points for every yes on this list:

1. The situation has the client as a major player in it.

2. The client can explore the topic freely.

3. The client could make a change that would appreciably affect the situation.

4. The client wants change.

5. The client is willing to try almost anything to get a change.

6. The client is ready to act right now.

7. The client is excited about imagining a change in this situation.

8. The client is willing and able to tell the coach what happened when he or she acted.

9. The client feels that the risk involved is manageable.

10. The coach is satisfied that the action under consideration is in the best interests of the client.

11. The action under consideration is within legal and ethical bounds, and will not legally jeopardize client or coach.

The Uncoachable Agenda

Subtract 10 points for every yes on this list:

1. The situation is dominated by another person who isn't willing to give up control.

2. The topic under consideration is something someone else needs to do.

3. The client feels completely powerless to change the situation and just wants to complain about it.

4. The client has already been working on this situation for months/years to little or no effect.

5. Circumstances require that the client put off taking action for weeks or months.

6. The agenda hasn't been set by the client.

7. The situation has negligible impact on the life or future of the client.

8. The client doesn't want to look at his or her impact on the situation.

9. The client is frightened of taking action.

10. The client is resigned to the possibility that nothing will change about the situation.

Coachability Index total: _____

If the total is less than 80 points, the agenda under consideration probably isn't worth spending time on. If this number seems high to you, consider that a master coach would never coach any topic that had less than a score of 90 on the first list or more than one yes on the second list.

Let's look at the individual elements of the index a little closer:

The Coachable Agenda

I. THE SITUATION HAS THE CLIENT AS A MAJOR PLAYER IN IT

Unless the client is directly involved in a situation, it is of little interest. Hearing about the wedding of the client's sister is probably a waste of coaching time. Coaching isn't conversation—the mundane details of the client's life should be weeded out of the coaching interaction, so the client stays focused on what's important in his own life. A coach can refocus a client by saying something like, "I don't think I need this information to coach you today. What's the one thing you want to focus on in today's session?"

2. THE CLIENT CAN EXPLORE THE TOPIC FREELY

Sometimes a client will call from work or some other place that isn't private enough to explore a topic thoroughly. If this is the case, the coach needs to urge the client to move to a setting in which she can talk freely.

Sometimes clients in corporate settings will fear sharing confidences because they aren't sure what the coach will do with this information. It is incumbent upon the coach to design an agreement with both the corporation and the individual that provides a level of confidentiality and transparency that every party understands and accepts.

3. THE CLIENT COULD MAKE A CHANGE THAT WOULD APPRECIABLY AFFECT THE SITUATION

If an individual feels like a victim—completely at the mercy of circumstances—no coaching can occur. If this belief is deep-seated, psychotherapy may be needed before the individual can become a coaching client. (Please read the section about blending practices in chapter 10 before deciding to fill both roles yourself.)

4. THE CLIENT WANTS CHANGE

As therapists, we've all worked with clients who don't really want to change their lives. A coach may have to ask a client hard questions to determine if this is the case—for example,

"What do you get out of keeping this situation unchanged?" and "What could go wrong if you changed this situation?"

5. THE CLIENT IS WILLING TO TRY ALMOST ANYTHING TO GET A CHANGE

Coaches need to be free to suggest bizarre homework—anything that might affect the situation. The client is always free to negotiate, but if a client rejects a coach's suggestions out of hand, without offering alternative homework, the client may not really want change.

6. THE CLIENT IS READY TO ACT RIGHT NOW

One of the primary functions of coaching is to support clients in implementing change. Although the generation of good ideas and action plans can be a stage in this process, the process isn't really begun until the client actually starts taking action. Insights, ten-page business plans, lists, and intentions mean nothing without action. If a client isn't ready to do something—anything!—in the next week to make things different, then the topic under consideration probably isn't coachable.

7. THE CLIENT IS EXCITED ABOUT IMAGINING A CHANGE IN THIS SITUATION

Coaches have to read the emotional tone of clients. If all the coach senses is dread, despair, resignation, or hopelessness, a client isn't likely to take effective action to change the situation—regardless of whether or not he accepts the coaching homework. A coachable client will be tossing out ideas and will jump to try something new.

8. THE CLIENT IS WILLING AND ABLE TO TELL THE COACH WHAT HAPPENED WHEN HE OR SHE ACTED

Action without reflection is just flailing around. A client needs to be willing to use coaching to evaluate the effectiveness of actions taken. Sometimes this means a coach will have to address the negative judgmental voices that interfere with a client's clarity in assessing the effectiveness of her actions. Sometimes a client will project this critical voice onto the coach; the coach then has to gently remove this projection, reassuring the client that he holds no judgment about the situation, only curiosity. (By the way, the coach must first self-manage to make sure he truly holds no judgment. Clients have well-honed lie detectors.)

9. THE CLIENT FEELS THAT THE RISK INVOLVED IS MANAGEABLE

An action plan that involves the possibility of physical injury, job loss, economic ruin, interpersonal disaster, emotional damage, or other dire consequence needs to be explored carefully, the risks involved fully assessed by the client. From there it's the client's call. Living life fully involves taking risks—in fact, that's part of the fun of it.

10. THE COACH IS SATISFIED THAT THE ACTION UNDER CONSIDERATION IS IN THE BEST INTERESTS OF THE CLIENT

This one is a tough call. Almost always, coaches will go with a client's call. After all, if we truly believe clients are creative, resourceful, and whole, then clients are the best judges of what is needed in their situations. Very occasionally, however, a coach will want to look at the long-term goals of the client and consider whether a short-term strategy is truly in alignment with the client's larger vision.

11. THE ACTION UNDER CONSIDERATION IS WITHIN LEGAL AND ETHICAL BOUNDS, AND WILL NOT LEGALLY OR ETHICALLY JEOPARDIZE CLIENT OR COACH

This is a veto issue. If a coach or client ever feels an action under consideration is in violation of their ethical, legal, or moral standards, either can simply say, "I'm not going along with that idea," or "I can't support you in that plan." If one of my clients wants to import cocaine in order to pay her debts, she'll have to find another coach.

The Uncoachable Agenda

1. THE SITUATION IS DOMINATED BY ANOTHER PERSON WHO ISN'T WILLING TO GIVE UP CONTROL

Tyrants exist in all walks of life; some are unavoidable. Coaching the victim of a tyrant will not change the tyrant. Coaches can only support clients in deciding what actions they can take within these onerous circumstances. If it's not in the best interests of the client to do anything, there is nothing that coaching can do to help.

2. THE TOPIC UNDER CONSIDERATION IS SOMETHING SOMEONE ELSE NEEDS TO DO

The coach cannot affect another person through the client. Talking about what someone else should do isn't coaching.

3. THE CLIENT FEELS COMPLETELY POWERLESS TO CHANGE THE SITUATION AND JUST WANTS TO COMPLAIN ABOUT IT

Some situations are simply unworkable. Sometimes circumstances dictate that a client cannot act until someone—or something—outside the client's control changes. If a client is unwilling or unable to act and his perspective about the situation is fixed, no coaching can be done.

We all want to complain about our lot in life. Complaining is appropriately done with friends and family; it's a waste of time in coaching.

4. THE CLIENT HAS ALREADY BEEN WORKING ON THIS SITUATION FOR MONTHS/YEARS TO LITTLE OR NO EFFECT

This one is a bit iffy. If a client really wants change, sometimes something the client has been working on for years can be cleared up in one session. This has happened enough times for me to know that it's not that unusual. But sometimes clients become more committed to having the problem than resolving it. For these clients, because coaching often highlights their unsuccessful attempts at change, coaching can be very frustrating. If, after a couple of months, a problem hasn't cleared up, the coach should consider whether the problem—but not necessarily the client—is uncoachable. If so, the client and coach can just agree not to work on that particular issue further.

5. CIRCUMSTANCES REQUIRE THAT THE CLIENT PUT OFF TAKING ACTION FOR WEEKS OR MONTHS

If a situation is coachable but can't be acted on until a later date, a coach and client may make a plan and simply delay implementation of it, moving on to agendas which can be addressed in the immediate future. But when a client only wants to talk about a situation she can do nothing about for months or years, it's a waste of both the coach's and the client's time.

6. THE AGENDA HASN'T BEEN SET BY THE CLIENT

Sometimes the person paying for the coaching isn't the person receiving it. This is common in corporate settings. If so, the coach needs to be very clear with both the client and the sponsor about who sets the agenda for the coaching. Often the sponsor's agenda and the client's agenda will be very different. It's not uncommon for a business to hire a coach to work with difficult employees and managers. If a client feels that coaching is just a prelude to being fired—or that it's an empty gesture on the part of the company—coaching is likely to be ineffectual.

7. THE SITUATION HAS NEGLIGIBLE IMPACT ON THE LIFE OR FUTURE OF THE CLIENT

Talking about dramatically pressing but irrelevant topics isn't coaching. This is exactly why coaches don't start sessions with "How are you?" Collecting tidbits of data about the current life of a client is a waste of time. If a client can't focus on a coaching topic that's relevant and important, the coach will have to stick with the client until together they find a coachable topic. The coach can say something like, "Look, just telling me what's going on with you isn't the best use of our time together. What specific issue would you like to focus on today?"

8. THE CLIENT DOESN'T WANT TO LOOK AT HIS OR HER IMPACT ON THE SITUATION

For all of us, it can be hard to see our part in a conflict at times. But when willful blindness is a persistent and pernicious pattern, a client may not be ready for coaching. Coaching requires a certain level of emotional intelligence—which includes a capacity for self-awareness, empathy, and insight. Some folks just don't have enough of these skills to be coached. Psychotherapy, adversity, or maturity can sometimes provide the cognitive and emotional experiences necessary for them to develop these skills.

9. THE CLIENT IS FRIGHTENED OF TAKING ACTION

Fears of taking action may be well-founded or self-generated. Either way, these fears can incapacitate a client, denying her the ability to creatively, proactively make choices. In these situations, coaching isn't the proper modality for the client; psychotherapy and cognitive approaches to anxiety management and/or phobic reactions may be needed.

10. THE CLIENT IS RESIGNED TO THE POSSIBILITY THAT NOTHING WILL CHANGE ABOUT THE SITUATION

Even if parts of a client's life are excluded from coaching, exciting coaching can still occur. I've had several clients tell me in intake sessions that their families are highly dysfunctional and they don't want any interaction with them. This is fine with me—we simply focus the coaching elsewhere. But if a client cannot successfully erect boundaries around these topics—but instead keeps returning to them with a depressed and hopeless emotional tone—psychotherapy or psychiatric intervention may be more appropriate than coaching.

THREE COACHING STRATEGIES

Before beginning the following self-coaching exercise, choose a topic in your own life that scores 100 or above on the Coachability Index. Think about your topic until you can frame it clearly and succinctly. Write it down.

The topic I want to be coached on is: _____

_____

_____

We're going to use three different approaches to work on this topic—three different ways of thinking about it as well as various strategies to arrive at an action plan. We'll begin with a linear approach:

Overcoming Obstacles

Whatever topic a client—you in this case—presents, there will always be obstacles to achieving the client's goal. How do we know that? Well, if the obstacles weren't there, the client would have already achieved the goal and wouldn't bring it to coaching! One way to work on a coaching topic is to examine these obstacles and design—and implement—a strategy to overcome them.

COACHING SKILL: Overcoming Obstacles

Goal: To analyze the existing obstacles to achieving a specific goal and develop and implement an action plan to overcome them.

Tool: Use the Overcoming Obstacles Worksheet to analyze and eliminate obstacles.

Since goal setting is a key element of this skill, before filling out the Overcoming Obstacles Worksheet, let's first look at some guidelines for framing effective goals:

GUIDELINES FOR GOALS

✓ Begin with the client. Have clients start goals with "I earn …" or "My team wins …" or "My company creates …"

✓ Phrase goals in the present tense, as though they've already been achieved. Don't say, "I want to buy a fancy new car," say, "I own a new BMW Z4."

✓ Make goals time-specific. For example, if it's January and the client's goal is to buy a BMW Z4 within the year, make the goal time-specific by phrasing it, "I own a new BMW Z4 that I bought in July of this year."

✓ Make goals concrete. "I demonstrate my ability to attract resources to me by purchasing the things I want" is pretty wimpy compared to "I own a new red BMW Z4 that I bought in July of this year." Vague abstractions are difficult to measure; clients can't celebrate successfully achieving them.

Use the following worksheet—add extra pages if necessary—to explore the specific obstacles to achieving your goal.

THE OVERCOMING OBSTACLES WORKSHEET

Identify a goal that's critical to dealing with the core of your coaching topic.

Goal: _____

Obstacles:

Identify the first three obstacles that must be surmounted in order to achieve this goal; identify which of the following three types of obstacles they are:

- External and environmental—e.g., finding financing, gathering materials, developing blueprints

- External and interpersonal—e.g., getting permission from a supervisor, putting together an effective sales team

- Internal—e.g., getting clear on a target market, overcoming doubts

List these obstacles in the order in which they need to be addressed, beginning with your very first obstacle.

Obstacle 1: _____

_____

Obstacle 2: _____

_____

Obstacle 3: _____

_____

Next, you'll develop a three-step action plan to address each of these obstacles. Think of three actions you can feasibly take that would improve the situation surrounding this obstacle. Write actions down in the order in which they should be achieved. Implement each of these actions, in order, and then use the space labeled "Evaluation" to assess the effectiveness of this action plan.

Action Plans:

OBSTACLE 1:

Action 1: _____

_____

Action 2: _____

_____

Action 3: _____

_____

Evaluation: _____

_____

OBSTACLE 2:

Action 1: _____

_____

Action 2: _____

_____

Action 3: _____

_____

Evaluation: _____

_____

OBSTACLE 3:

Action 1: _____

_____

Action 2: _____

_____

Action 3: _____

_____

Evaluation: _____

_____

After implementing these action plans, what's your next step? _____

_____

_____

_____

_____

_____

The following is a truncated example of a completed worksheet:

THE OVERCOMING OBSTACLES WORKSHEET EXAMPLE

Goal: *In December of this year I am offered a three-book deal from my publisher.*

Obstacles:

Obstacle 1: *External and environmental: Sales figures on current books must improve. What can I do to influence this?*

Obstacle 2: *External and interpersonal: Relationships with my publishing house decision-makers must be enthusiastically positive. Previous interactions with them have been spotty; I haven't been treating them as my most important client.*

Obstacle 3: *Internal: I must put my writing above everything else. My need to take care of others has been getting in the way of my putting my career first.*

Action Plans:

OBSTACLE 1: *External and environmental: Sales figures on current books must improve.*

Action 1: *Contact book clubs and send flyers.*

Action 2: *Develop an alliance with another author to assist with marketing.*

Action 3: *Write personal letters to key booksellers.*

Evaluation: *Did all three. For the last four months sales went up an average of 22 percent per month.*

OBSTACLE 2: *External and interpersonal: Relationships with my publishing house decision-makers must be enthusiastically positive.*

Action 1: *Meet face-to-face with three top decision-makers.*

Action 2: *Send three e-mails to my publishing house's executives, celebrating the successes of my book.*

Action 3: *Get three press releases published that feature my publisher and distribute them to all the key decision-makers in the publishing house.*

Evaluation: *Did actions 1 and 2, but only got one press release published. Impact: got several enthusiastic responses, and the house paid $1,000 to bookstores to promote my book—very unusual for them.*

OBSTACLE 3: *Internal: I must put my writing above everything else.*

Action1: *Talk to my wife and get her buy-in on this.*

Action 2: *Set up a weekly writing schedule, with writing days blocked out.*

Action 3: *Schedule writing retreat.*

Evaluation: *Did actions 1 and 2. Finished my manuscript ahead of schedule.*

What's my next step? *Publisher isn't willing to do more than a two-book deal. Still, that's progress. I need to reevaluate.*

Discovering New Perspectives

Another way to tackle a coaching topic is to explore how the client could open himself to other perspectives of the issue. Often a situation will seem problematic simply because we're considering it from a limited perspective. In coaching we can reframe issues—sometimes making previously perceived obstacles and difficulties just melt away. Let's try it:

COACHING SKILL: Discovering New Perspectives
(This skill blends together imagery, linear thinking, and strategizing.)

Goal: To see other perspectives of a situation.

Tool: Use the New Perspectives Worksheet to open up new options for yourself.

THE NEW PERSPECTIVES WORKSHEET

You are about to enter the Mansion of Possibilities. To do this, you have to be willing to play and use your imagination a little. Some folks will find this very easy; others will get a little frustrated. Hang in there and see what you learn.

In a few simple sentences, describe the situation you currently find yourself in. _____

_____

_____

Next, imagine that this perspective is only one of several perspectives that you could hold. Think of this perspective as a room in a mansion. Would the perspective you hold be best depicted as a dusty basement, a lush bedroom, an abandoned attic, a messy kitchen, or some other room? What room would best depict the view you currently hold of your situation? Describe this room, including the furniture in it, the view out the window, the color of the walls, the smell, and any other details you imagine. Have fun painting a word picture of it:

_____

_____

_____

How does this room portray your current beliefs? (For example, your answer might be something like, "The painting of wildflowers on the wall reminds me of planting seeds to make my project grow. I need to see myself as a gardener, not just a salesperson.") _____

_____

Okay, now imagine another room in the mansion. Just pick one at random and walk right in. This new room depicts an entirely different way you could view the set of circumstances you find yourself in. Is it a kid's toy room, a pantry, a library, or some other completely unexpected room? Describe it: _____

_____

_____

Now, from inside this new room, ask yourself, "What can this room teach me about how to understand my situation in a completely new way, from a completely different perspective?" Write down what you learn:

_____

_____

Time for room number three. Let this room really surprise you—it can be anywhere in the mansion. Just open the door, go inside, and describe what you see and experience: _____

_____

_____

_____

How would the way you look at and handle your situation differ in this new room? _____

_____

We'll enter room number four differently: try to think of another way to understand and manage the circumstances you find yourself in—something you haven't thought of before. Now imagine a room to express this new perspective. Describe this room: _____

_____

_____

_____

Now you have four rooms, each depicting a different way to look at your situation. The first room represents the box you usually find yourself in on this topic. Choose one of the three new rooms you've discovered. This is the room you will live in for the next week. Walk into it in your imagination. Look around, settle in. From this new perspective, what three specific actions are you going to take this week—actions that you would never have dreamed of taking when you were stuck in that first room?

Action 1: _____

_____

Action 2: _____

_____

Action 3: _____

_____

THE NEW PERSPECTIVES WORKSHEET EXAMPLE

The writer who did the Overcoming Obstacles Worksheet also tried this one. Here were his results:

The room I lived in for a week was actually the coal room. It was dark and dirty—but very warm since it was right next to the furnace. I couldn't see anything, so my first action step was to send a personal letter to someone on my contact list whom I didn't know, and whom I couldn't see being able to help me much. I just sort of blindly reached out, like I would in the coal room. It turned out she was the sister of a Hollywood agent, to whom I then sent a pitch for my book. I don't know what will happen with that.

The second really noticeable thing about the coal room was how dirty it was. So that week I cleaned out my desk and working area—and found an outline for a short story that I'd totally forgotten about.

The third thing about that room was that it was warm. I got my hot tub fixed, and now I soak every night. I'm doing the stretches my doctor suggested while soaking. This is really helping me with the mild carpal tunnel pain that I've been struggling with.

Good job! You now have more action plans than you ever wanted. Next, go back and review the topic you started with. After you've reviewed it, let's try the last of these three coaching approaches:

Working Backwards

COACHING SKILL: Working from the Solution Backwards

(This one combines a bit of imagination and a bit of advice giving.)

Goal: To help the client develop an internal ally in strategizing.

Tool: Use the Magic Telephone exercise to discover advice perfectly tailored to you.

THE MAGIC TELEPHONE

Imagine that you've been given a magic telephone. Its magic is quite specific: this magic telephone connects the present with the future. In just a minute this telephone is going to ring and you'll be talking to yourself, a few months in the future. The good news is that the situation that you're currently worried about has worked out perfectly, thanks to your skillful actions. The bad news is that your future self will only have a short time to give you exactly the pithy advice you need to handle the next couple of weeks.

The phone rings. Pick it up and listen to the good advice. You'll be told exactly what you need to do next to handle this situation and achieve your goal.

Write down the advice you receive: _____

_____

YOUR COACHING HOMEWORK

Having coached yourself extensively, it's now time for action. Review all of the previous material and assign yourself three actions you will take—without fail—in the next week to address your coaching topic. Write them down right now; check off and date each action when it is completed.

ACTION PLAN FOR THE NEXT WEEK

Goal I want to accomplish in the next week: _____

_____

Action 1: _____

    Completed: ____/____/____

Action 2: _____

    Completed: ____/____/____

Action 3: _____

    Completed: ____/____/____

CHAPTER TEN

LEGAL, ADMINISTRATIVE, & ETHICAL ISSUES

In this chapter we'll look at a collection of issues that arise when you add coaching to your current practice. First of all, let's consider the legal issues—and avoid lawsuits!

LEGAL ISSUES

As far as I know, coaching as a profession has—so far—been relatively untouched by extensive lawsuits. Since large insurance companies aren't involved in coaching there are no deep pockets for plaintiffs and their lawyers to pursue.

However, there are a variety of different legal issues that can arise with coaching; these include the dangers of a blended practice, coaching contracts, confidentiality, mandates to report, and the boundary between therapy and coaching.

The Dangers of a Blended Practice

Let me begin by uttering a ritual phrase that you will use often as a coach—one that I am using right now as author of this book: "I have no professional expertise in this area [law, in this case] and my opinions are those of a member of the general public. I recommend you consult a professional in this area [e.g., a lawyer] to get a professional opinion about these matters."

Good, with that out of the way, I can now talk about the problems of mixing coaching and therapy. I could make this section very short and just say, "Don't do it." But it seems useful to explain why.

On the surface it seems an appealing idea. As therapists, we know that the distinctions between therapy and coaching set down in the early chapters aren't entirely reflective of actual experience. The world can't really be neatly divided into two separate categories of people: those who are mentally ill and need therapy and those who are mentally healthy but could benefit from coaching. Some therapy clients actually have greater mental health than their therapists. Some very neurotic folks benefit greatly from coaching. Some folks oscillate between mental health and mental illness; everyone does the occasional tour through the dark side of their psyche.

A therapist who has stewarded a client through hard times seems the perfect person to also see this client into the land of fulfillment, satisfaction, and success. The trust between the two would be solid—and the context the therapist-coach would bring to the work rich. The combination may work well for all concerned. But what happens if it doesn't?

Numerous books, articles, and legal opinions focus on the potential harmful effects to the client from these dual relationships. That isn't my concern in this section—I'm concerned about the harmful effects of these dual relationships on the therapist-coach. And, in my unprofessional legal opinion, these effects can be severe.

Therapists can purchase liability insurance and are provided some privacy protection under the law. However, these protections may be voided by blending therapy and coaching. Even assuming that as a therapist-coach you get your client to sign a contract stating that from this point on you're in a coaching relationship, this boundary is open to legal challenge.

Every therapist who has practiced for a few years has had clients whom they have misdiagnosed. We're human, we make mistakes. However, in blending practices we risk invalidating the structures that have evolved to protect us when we make mistakes as therapists. We also risk losing our licenses and place everything—including our financial security—in jeopardy of a lawsuit.

A final caveat: don't bill insurance companies for coaching services. If you do, prepare to go to prison. Billing insurance companies for coaching is both illegal and unethical. Coaching has never been covered by insurance and doesn't want to be covered by insurance. After seeing what has happened to therapy—where length of treatment is now determined as much by a distant insurance bureaucrat as it is by the treating professional—the coaching profession has developed a well-founded distrust of insurance companies.

So what's the alternative to blending your practices? Simple: coach your coaching clients and give therapy to your therapy clients—and don't mix them. Refer clients to others if they need other services; don't provide them yourself.

Coaching Contracts

As a therapist, you should already have a contract specifying the range and limitations of your therapeutic work. Create a similar contract for your coaching, specifically stating that you will not be doing any form of psychotherapy with clients.

The following is the contract I use. It's meant as an example, not the Magna Carta:

COACHING AGREEMENT

This **agreement** between **Coach:** David Skibbins and **Client:** _____ will begin on **Date:** _____ and will continue for a minimum of three months. The fee for the two-hour initial intake session is **$350.00** and the fee per month is **$350.00**, payable monthly in advance. A month's worth of coaching shall consist of three half-hour sessions.

The services to be provided by **Coach** to the **Client** are face-to-face coaching or telecoaching, as designed jointly with the client, supplemented as needed and agreed upon by both parties with e-mail communication. Coaching, which is not advice, therapy, or counseling, may address specific personal projects, goals, issues of life balance, business successes, or general conditions in the client's life or profession. Other coaching services or activities may include values clarification, brainstorming, personal strategic planning, and work on perspective in order to broaden the client's understanding of the choices the client faces. Coaching may involve all areas of a client's personal and professional life.

Even though David Skibbins is licensed as a Marriage and Family Counselor in the State of California, his coaching does not include the rendering of psychotherapeutic advice or services, and no therapist-client relationship is created or implied by this agreement. Coaching does not involve either the diagnosis of mental illness or its treatment. It is not a substitute for professional counseling, psychotherapy, treatment for addiction issues, or marital and family therapy. If you are currently in therapy, your therapist must be made aware that you are a coaching client as well as a therapy client.

The **Client** and **Coach** agree to provide one another with 30-day notice in the event either party desires to cancel services.

As your coach, I, David Skibbins, promise you that all information shared with me will be kept strictly confidential, except as required by law. Sometimes information that you share with me may be specific and explicitly personal. Your willingness to be truthful will be treated with the ultimate respect, as a special confidence. At the conclusion of our work together, all written records of our work will be destroyed to preserve your privacy.

Throughout our working relationship our conversations will be direct and personal. You can count on me to be honest and straightforward, ask clarifying questions, make empowering requests, and assign creative, useful homework. The purpose of our interaction is to hold your focus on your desired outcome and to coach you to stay clear, focused, and in action.

By signing below, the **Coach** and the **Client** agree to keep these agreements and appointments; the **Client** agrees to keep the **Coach** informed as to what is needed to keep the process moving forward. In the event that you, the **Client**, are dissatisfied, please discuss with me what you need.

Our signatures on this agreement indicate full understanding of and agreement with the information outlined above.

_____   _____
Coach   Date

_____   _____
Client   Date

For another take on the coaching contract, BELOW is a contract taken from the website of the International Coach Federation (www.coachfederation.org):

SAMPLE COACHING AGREEMENT

This is one sample of an agreement. It is not intended to be the only type of agreement.

Coach's name: _____

Coach's address: _____

To my client: Please review, adjust, sign where indicated, and return to me at the above address.

CLIENT'S NAME _____

INITIAL TERM _____ MONTHS, FROM _____ THROUGH _____

FEE $_____ PER MONTH, $ _____ FOR THE PROJECT

SESSION DAY _____ SESSION TIME _____

NUMBER OF SESSIONS PER MONTH _____

DURATION _____ (length of scheduled session)

REFERRED BY: _____

GROUND RULES:
1. CLIENT CALLS THE COACH AT THE SCHEDULED TIME.
2. CLIENT PAYS COACHING FEES IN ADVANCE.
3. CLIENT PAYS FOR LONG-DISTANCE CHARGES, IF ANY.

1. As a client, I understand and agree that I am fully responsible for my physical, mental, and emotional well-being during my coaching calls, including my choices and decisions. I am aware that I can choose to discontinue coaching at any time.

2. I understand that "coaching" is a Professional-Client relationship I have with my coach that is designed to facilitate the creation/development of personal, professional, or business goals and to develop and carry out a strategy/plan for achieving those goals.

3. I understand that coaching is a comprehensive process that may involve all areas of my life, including work, finances, health, relationships, education, and recreation. I acknowledge that deciding how to handle these issues, incorporate coaching into those areas, and implement my choices is exclusively my responsibility.

---

4. I understand that coaching does not involve the diagnosis or treatment of mental disorders as defined by the American Psychiatric Association. I understand that coaching is not a substitute for counseling, psychotherapy, psychoanalysis, mental health care, or substance abuse treatment and I will not use it in place of any form of diagnosis, treatment, or therapy.

5. I promise that if I am currently in therapy or otherwise under the care of a mental health professional, that I have consulted with the mental health care provider regarding the advisability of working with a coach and that this person is aware of my decision to proceed with the coaching relationship.

6. I understand that information will be held as confidential unless I state otherwise, in writing, except as required by law.

7. I understand that certain topics may be anonymously and hypothetically shared with other coaching professionals for training OR consultation purposes.

8. I understand that coaching is not to be used as a substitute for professional advice by legal, medical, financial, business, spiritual, or other qualified professionals. I will seek independent professional guidance for legal, medical, financial, business, spiritual, or other matters. I understand that all decisions in these areas are exclusively mine and I acknowledge that my decisions and my actions regarding them are my sole responsibility.

I have read and agree to the above.

_____
                       Client Signature

_____
             Date

Now it's your turn. Use the two contracts above—as well as any client contracts and guidelines you currently use for psychotherapy—to design your own coaching contract.

COACHING SKILL: Designing Your Contract

Goal: To define the legal structure of your working relationship with your coaching clients.

Tool: Use the Creating Your Coaching Contract exercise to create your customized contract.

CREATING YOUR COACHING CONTRACT

1.   Take out a fresh sheet of paper (or turn on the computer).

2.   Write down bullet points of what you'll want to cover in your coaching contract.

3.   Cut and paste from the contract you currently use as a psychotherapist—and from any other source you find helpful. (Enter "coaching contracts" into Google and you'll discover many examples.)

4.   Draw up your coaching contract from this material and your bullet points. There's no one correct way, so focus on making it work for you and your circumstances.

Confidentiality

As therapists, we tend to have extensive experience at maintaining clinical confidentiality, both in our personal interactions and regarding our clinical records. Some of this experience is directly transferable. However, the world of coaching is much more amorphous than the well-established world of psychotherapy. For instance, when we are hired by a company to coach its employees, who will have access to coaching information? Coaches have to continually make clear the boundaries of their confidentiality.

The International Coach Federation (ICF) directly addresses issues of confidentiality in several of its ethical guidelines, published on its website (www.coachfederation.org; the ICF's complete code of ethics is included later in this chapter):

8. I will accurately create, maintain, store, and dispose of any records of work done in relation to the practice of coaching in a way that promotes confidentiality and complies with any applicable laws.

13. I will ensure that, prior to or at the initial session, my coaching client understands the nature of coaching, the bounds of confidentiality, financial arrangements, and other terms of the coaching agreement.

22. I will respect the confidentiality of my client's information, except as otherwise authorized by my client, or as required by law.

23. I will obtain agreement from my clients before releasing their names as clients or references, or any other client-identifying information.

24. I will obtain agreement from the person being coached before releasing information to another person compensating me.

These guidelines are much looser than the ones we maintain for our therapy practices. I believe that it behooves a therapist to maintain even more stringent confidentiality guidelines than the ones established by the ICF for coaches, particularly in regard to both the security of records and the sharing of client information.

SECURING RECORDS

Maintain your coaching records in a secure, locked place, with the same safeguards against theft or hacking that you maintain for clinical records. Intimate information is contained in these records—we need to secure the privacy of all of our clients.

When a client is involved in a lawsuit, issues of client records, confidentiality, and privileged communication start to loom. As coaches, we have even less ability to protect our records than we do as therapists. In my opinion, coaches have no legal basis for asserting privilege in regard to these records because there is, as of yet, no case law that supports this. I believe a subpoena gets all written coaching information. (Although the verbal communications between us and our clients may be considered hearsay, any written information will probably be admissible.)

Three options exist to address this situation:

Option 1: Don't take records.

I stopped taking client notes after my case notes as a psychotherapist got subpoenaed in a custody case. Since not taking notes violates standard psychotherapy practice, this choice would have reflected negatively on my professionalism as a therapist had I ever again been called to testify. There are no standards for practice in reference to note-taking as a coach, so choosing this option is perfectly acceptable.

Option 2: Maintain records.

Remember, hard disks can now be confiscated, so the fact that your records are paperless offers you no protection. In this modern world of increasing police powers assume that your records are available to any law enforcement authorities any time they want to peruse them. Make entries accordingly.

Option 3: At the end of the coaching contract return all records to the client.

This is often a nice gesture, as it provides the client with a record of your work together. It also leaves you with nothing to be discovered under a subpoena.

SHARING CLIENT INFORMATION

Unlike therapy, coaching in a corporate environment is often paid for by a client's employer. In this situation the need to maintain client confidentiality becomes even more stringent than in the situation more commonly faced as a therapist—i.e., the need to maintain client confidentiality in dealing with insurance reimbursement. In corporate settings, confidentiality issues are worse as a coach. In the coaching setting, the person who has direct hiring and firing power over your client is often the person you have to report to about the results of the coaching. In terms of liability issues, a good rule of thumb to remember is that you're unlikely to be sued for underreporting client information, but you could be sued for overreporting client information.

I tell both my potential employer and my potential client my policy about sharing client information: I make it a rule to vet all communications I intend to have with a client's employer with the client first. The client has the final veto about what gets communicated and what doesn't.

This rule takes me out of a parental role and places me squarely in the camp of the client. Some companies don't hire me because of this stance; however, I maintain it because it keeps me from becoming a pawn in the internal politics of a company. If a company wants to fire an employee, they won't do it by hiring me to inform on that employee.

The Problem of Mandates to Report

So far, mandates to report abuse and potential to harm don't apply to the coaching profession. However, when a licensed therapist hears reports of abuse from a coaching client, there are still ethical—and perhaps legal—ramifications to be considered. This is an unexplored swamp. The good news is that I've never run into a situation in coaching which would require reporting. Coaching clients tend to be more responsible than therapy clients.

To address the problem more directly, I contemplated putting a paragraph into my contract that would read:

"As my client, you understand that, while I have no legal mandate to report child or elder abuse, as your coach I expect that you will do something to stop it. If authorities need to intervene, the two of us will design how best to have that happen."

However, in the end the wording of this warning just seemed too grim for a coaching contract. Whether or not to include such language is your decision. In my experience, reporting abuse isn't an issue most coaches have to struggle with.

The Boundary Between Therapy and Coaching

A non-clinically trained coach may, understandably, have a difficult time understanding the demarcation between therapy and coaching. The ICF has published guidelines on its website (www.coachfederation.org) to help clarify when nonclinicians should bring in professional help. These guidelines are good reminders for all coaches—even those trained as therapists.

Top Ten Indicators to Refer to a Mental Health Professional

Your client:

1. Is exhibiting a decline in his/her ability to experience pleasure and/or an increase in being sad, hopeless, and helpless.

    - As a coach you may notice that your client is not as upbeat as usual.

    - He/she may talk much more frequently about how awful life/the world is and that nothing can be done about it.

    - The client may make comments about "why bother" or "what's the use."

    - There will be a decline in talking about things that are enjoyable.

    - He/she may stop doing things they like to do (examples: going to the movies, visiting with friends, participating in athletic events, or being a spectator at sporting events).

    - The client begins to talk about being unable to do anything that forwards their dreams or desires.

2. Has intrusive thoughts or is unable to concentrate or focus.

    - As a coach you may notice that your client is not able to focus on goals or on the topic of conversation.

    - The client is unable to complete action steps and isn't aware of what got in the way.

    - You notice that your client begins talking about unpleasant events during the course of talking about goals, or while talking about himself/herself.

    - The client tells you that unpleasant thoughts keep popping into mind at inopportune moments or when the client is thinking about or doing other things, and that it seems impossible to get away from these thoughts.

    - Your client tells you about recurring scary dreams that didn't occur before.

    - Your client reports that there are so many thoughts swirling in his or her head, and that the client can't get the thoughts to slow down.

3. Is unable to get to sleep, or awakens during the night and is unable to get back to sleep, or sleeps excessively.

    - Your client comes to coaching sessions tired and exhausted.

    - Your client begins talking about not being able to get to sleep or how he/she just wants to sleep all the time.

- Your client may report to you how he/she gets to sleep and then wakes up and can't get back to sleep.

- Your client tells of needing to take naps during the day, and that this is new.

- Your client reports falling asleep at an inopportune time or place.

4. Has a change in appetite: decrease in appetite or increase in appetite.

   - Your client reports that he/she isn't hungry and just doesn't want to eat.

   - Your client reports that he/she is eating all the time, usually sweets or junk food, even without feeling hungry.

   - Your client says that there's no enjoyment to be gotten from eating although there was in the past.

   - Your client reports not sitting down to eat with friends or family and that this is a new development.

5. Is feeling guilty because others have suffered or died.

   - Your client reports feeling guilty because he/she is alive or has not been injured.

   - Your client can't understand why he/she is still here, still alive when others have had to suffer/die.

   - Your client doesn't want to move forward on goals; doesn't feel deserving of the life the client chooses, especially when other people have had to suffer/die.

   - Your client questions the right to have a fulfilling life/career in the face of all that has happened.

   - Your client expresses the belief that he/she is unworthy of having a satisfying life.

6. Has feelings of despair or hopelessness.

   - According to your client, nothing in life is OK.

   - Your client misses session times or expresses the desire to quit coaching because life is not worth living, or because the client feels undeserving of getting what he/she wants.

   - Your client moves into excessive negative thinking.

   - Your client says that it's impossible to make a difference or that whatever he/she does doesn't matter.

   - Your client has the attitude "Why bother?"

7. Is being hyperalert and/or excessively tired.

   - Your client reports an inability to relax.
   - Your client states that he/she jumps at the slightest noise.
   - Your client reports a need to be always on guard.
   - Your client reports listening for any little sound that is out of the ordinary.
   - Your client reports a lack of energy.
   - Your client describes an inability to do their usual chores because of being so tired.
   - Your client tells you that it takes too much energy to do things that were once normal routine.

8. Has increased irritability or outbursts of anger.

   - Your client becomes increasingly belligerent or argumentative with you or other people.
   - Your client reports that everyone or everything is annoying.
   - Your client starts making comments about how miserable everyone and everything is.
   - Your client reports that other people are saying how miserable/angry the client has become.
   - Your client reports getting into arguments with people.
   - Your client tells of getting so upset that "I don't know what to do with myself."
   - Your client reports feeling like a "pressure cooker" or being "ready to burst."
   - Your client increasingly tells you about wanting to do or doing things that would harm the client or others (examples: wanting to put a fist through a window; wanting to punch someone; wanting to run into someone/something in a car).

9. Has impulsive and risk-taking behavior.

   - Your client reports doing things, such as going on a buying spree, without thinking about the consequences.
   - Your client tells you that something came to mind, so he/she went and did it without thinking about the outcome.
   - Your client reports an increase in doing things that could be detrimental to the client or others (examples: increase in promiscuous sexual behavior; increase

in alcohol/drug consumption; deciding to get married after knowing someone an unusually short period of time).

10. Has thoughts of death and/or suicide.

- Your client begins talking a lot about death, not just a fear of dying.

- Your client alludes to the fact that dying would be appropriate for him/her.

- Your client makes comments that to die right now would be OK.

- Your client becomes fascinated with what dying would be like.

- Your client talks about ways to die.

- Your client talks about going to a better place and how wonderful it would be and seems to be carried away by the thought.

- Your client tells you he/she knows how they would kill themselves if they wanted to/had the chance.

- Your client alludes to having a plan or way to die/go to a better place/leave the planet/leave the situation/get out of here.

- Whereas previously your client was engaging, personable, and warm, now he/she presents to you as cold, distant, and aloof.

Some questions you might ask your client if you are unclear about what is going on: "Are you wanting to die?" "How would you die if you decided to?" "Are you planning on dying?" "When are you planning on dying?"

If you have any inclination or indication that your client is planning on dying/suiciding, immediately refer the client to an emergency room or call 911. Tell your client that you care about him/her, are concerned for him/her, that you are taking what he/she says seriously and that he/she must get help immediately. If the client balks at what you are saying, gets belligerent, or more distant, AND you become even more concerned, you may need to say that you will break confidentiality because of your concern and that you will call 911. (You can call your local 911 and give them the address and phone number of your client, even if it is in another state, and they can contact the client's local 911 dispatcher.)

It is important to note that the appearance of any one of these indicators, except for #10 which must be referred and followed up on immediately, does not indicate the immediate need for a referral to a psychotherapist or community mental health agency; anyone can experience a very brief episode of any of the indicators. However, if you see that several indicators are emerging and that the client is not presenting as whole, competent, and capable then it is time for a referral to a mental health professional.

The coach who is also a trained therapist is in a much more difficult position. As therapists, we can address many of these issues directly and effectively—sometimes giving clinical advice that can immediately assist clients. And yet, every time we do that we blur the boundary between therapy and coaching. Even though we may have very clear written contracts and verbal understandings with our coaching clients that coaching is not therapy, we can undermine these agreements with comments like the following:

"Have you tried time-outs with your little boy?"

"Stick with the medication your doctor prescribed; often antidepressants take a few weeks to build up to a therapeutic level in the bloodstream."

"Your wife sounds like she may have an addiction issue, and may need professional help."

"This is a stress reduction technique that has worked well with some of my clients."

"I'm detecting some resistance from you about what I just said."

"I wonder if your boss is projecting his mother issues onto you."

When a non-clinically trained coach makes comments like these, a client can simply decide if they're true for her. However, the fact that you have clinical training as a therapist automatically places you in a position of authority. Thus, psychologically descriptive language and opinions will be given a great deal of weight by your clients if you offer them. Furthermore, by showing up as the expert—even in this subtle way—you'll be undermining your clients' own sense of autonomy and authority.

The best strategy in circumstances in which you feel psychological help is needed is to refer out. Your clients will appreciate your ethical boundaries and professionalism—and as a result will take your recommendation all the more seriously. Making such a referral looks something like this:

"Fred, I've been your coach now for three months, and a persistent source of suffering for you seems to be your ongoing arguments with your wife. Coaching can't really help with this issue. I think the two of you need some professional counseling to learn how to get what you want out of your relationship. If you want, I can give you a list of three counselors whose work I respect."

As a clinically trained coach, it is incumbent upon you to manage your language even more thoroughly than a non-clinically trained coach has to. If you conscientiously weed out psychological jargon and refrain from offering interpretations and psychological advice, you will have a clear boundary between your two practices—something both you and your clients will benefit from.

ADMINISTRATIVE ISSUES

In the next chapter we'll explore tools and techniques for attracting clients to your door. But before you open that door, you have some additional administrative decisions to make. (You may have visited some of these already if you have a private practice or have run another small business.)

COACHING SKILL: Starting Your Own Coaching Business

Goal: To determine and accomplish the steps needed to set up the administrative structure of your coaching business.

Tool: Use the Start Your Own Coaching Business Checklist to tackle administrative issues before implementing your marketing plan.

Checklists like the following—customized for therapists starting their own coaching businesses—are a great tool for anyone beginning a major undertaking.

START YOUR OWN COACHING BUSINESS CHECKLIST: THINGS TO DO BEFORE IMPLEMENTING YOUR MARKETING PLAN

❑ Choose a business name for your coaching business that's separate from any business identity you may have as a therapist. Sometimes it's enough to just make new cards: David Skibbins, Ph.D., PCC, Coach versus David Skibbins, Ph.D., MFCC.

❑ See if this business name is available as a domain name. Reserve it now! This will be very handy for your website later on. You don't have to get cute—e.g., www.davidskibbins.com is fine.

❑ Verify your right to use this business name. In many areas, if you name your business something other than your own name, you have to file a fictitious name statement with the county or state.

❑ Get a local business license, one that's separate from your psychotherapy practice, specifying that it is exclusively for coaching and consulting.

❑ Choose a place of business. Using your home address for your coaching practice instead of your therapy office will further buttress distinctions between your practice as a coach and your practice as a therapist. Make sure you comply with local zoning laws.

❑ Have an extra phone line installed for your coaching calls.

❏ Check into malpractice or errors-and-omission insurance for your coaching practice, if available. You may be able to add a rider to your current therapy liability insurance to include coaching. Your therapy insurance will not, however, automatically cover your coaching, too. In rare cases insurers have dropped therapists from their rolls when therapists added coaching to their menu of services, so be sure you speak with your insurer to make certain you're covered for your new profession.

❏ Open a bank account for your coaching business that's separate from any account you have for your therapy practice. This will further delineate the separateness of these two enterprises.

❏ Have business cards and stationery printed.

❏ Purchase a really good headset. (Plantronics makes an excellent one.)

❏ Set up a records system to track clients, referral sources, and potential clients.

❏ Set up a client invoicing system to manage billing and track payments.

Work on your marketing plan should continue apace with pinning down these administrative tasks. (See chapter 11 for more information about developing a marketing plan.)

ETHICAL ISSUES

It may seem odd to some of you that I've put ethics last in this chapter. I've done so because many therapists will already have grappled with thorny ethical issues in their own practices. It's a conversation we're already well versed in. Ethical considerations are part of our training, and the continuing education necessary to renew our licenses keeps us up-to-date on these issues.

The following are the ethical guidelines of the coaching industry, as set down by the International Coach Federation on its website (www.coachfederation.org):

The ICF Standards of Ethical Conduct

Professional Conduct at Large

As a coach:

1. I will conduct myself in a manner that reflects positively upon the coaching profession and I will refrain from engaging in conduct or making statements that may negatively impact the public's understanding or acceptance of coaching as a profession.

2. I will not knowingly make any public statements that are untrue or misleading, or make false claims in any written documents relating to the coaching profession.

3. I will respect different approaches to coaching. I will honor the efforts and contributions of others and not misrepresent them as my own.

4. I will be aware of any issues that may potentially lead to the misuse of my influence by recognizing the nature of coaching and the way in which it may affect the lives of others.

5. I will at all times strive to recognize personal issues that may impair, conflict, or interfere with my coaching performance or my professional relationships. Whenever the facts and circumstances necessitate, I will promptly seek professional assistance and determine the action to be taken, including whether it is appropriate to suspend or terminate my coaching relationship(s).

6. As a trainer or supervisor of current and potential coaches, I will conduct myself in accordance with the ICF Code of Ethics in all training and supervisory situations.

7. I will conduct and report research with competence, honesty, and within recognized scientific standards. My research will be carried out with the necessary approval or consent from those involved, and with an approach that will reasonably protect participants from any potential harm. All research efforts will be performed in a manner that complies with the laws of the country in which the research is conducted.

8. I will accurately create, maintain, store, and dispose of any records of work done in relation to the practice of coaching in a way that promotes confidentiality and complies with any applicable laws.

9. I will use ICF member contact information (email addresses, telephone numbers, etc.) only in the manner and to the extent authorized by the ICF.

Professional Conduct with Clients

10. I will be responsible for setting clear, appropriate, and culturally sensitive boundaries that govern any physical contact that I may have with my clients.

11. I will not become sexually involved with any of my clients.

12. I will construct clear agreements with my clients, and will honor all agreements made in the context of professional coaching relationships.

13. I will ensure that, prior to or at the initial session, my coaching client understands the nature of coaching, the bounds of confidentiality, financial arrangements, and other terms of the coaching agreement.

14. I will accurately identify my qualifications, expertise, and experience as a coach.

15. I will not intentionally mislead or make false claims about what my client will receive from the coaching process or from me as their coach.

16. I will not give my clients or prospective clients information or advice I know or believe to be misleading.

17. I will not knowingly exploit any aspect of the coach-client relationship for my personal, professional, or monetary advantage or benefit.

18. I will respect the client's right to terminate coaching at any point during the process. I will be alert to indications that the client is no longer benefiting from our coaching relationship.

19. If I believe the client would be better served by another coach, or by another resource, I will encourage the client to make a change.

20. I will suggest that my clients seek the services of other professionals when deemed appropriate or necessary.

21. I will take all reasonable steps to notify the appropriate authorities in the event a client discloses an intention to endanger self or others.

Confidentiality/Privacy

22. I will respect the confidentiality of my client's information, except as otherwise authorized by my client, or as required by law.

23. I will obtain agreement from my clients before releasing their names as clients or references, or any other client-identifying information.

24. I will obtain agreement from the person being coached before releasing information to another person compensating me.

Conflicts of Interest

25. I will seek to avoid conflicts between my interests and the interests of my clients.

26. Whenever any actual conflict of interest or the potential for a conflict of interest arises, I will openly disclose it and fully discuss with my client how to deal with it in whatever way best serves my client.

27. I will disclose to my client all anticipated compensation from third parties that I may receive for referrals of that client.

28. I will only barter for services, goods, or other non-monetary remuneration when it will not impair the coaching relationship.

These standards offer a clear ethical backbone for the profession. Many coaches print this code of ethics out and include it in their intake packages, so that clients know both that coaching has ethical guidelines and exactly what those guidelines are.

CHAPTER ELEVEN

ESTABLISHING A MARKETING PLAN

It's not enough to decide you want to be a coach and do the administrative tasks necessary to set up a business. You also need coaching clients! Where do you get them? In this chapter we'll create a powerful marketing plan perfectly tailored to your needs and circumstances. There will be no three-fold brochures, no expensive mailings, no high-cost advertising campaigns—it will all be done through relationships.

By the end of this chapter you will have clear, strong answers to the following five questions:

1.   How do you describe your services?

2.   What do you charge?

3.   Whom do you target?

4.   What do you need to do to implement this marketing plan?

5.   How do you differentiate yourself from other coaches?

HOW DO YOU DESCRIBE YOUR SERVICES?

This one is easy now. We've already learned exactly what coaching is and how to distinguish between therapy and coaching. Now, please forget all of these elegant distinctions! Rather than describe your services, give a potential client a sample of your work—a test drive rather than a brochure. "What's coaching? Let me show you." It has been years since I described what coaching is to a potential client. If you ask potential clients to save their questions until after the coaching sample, nine out of ten times the only questions you'll be asked will be logistical: when, for how long, and how much.

However, you do need a single sentence that describes your services in terms of the ideal client you want to serve. This is called an *elevator speech*—a short description of your job you could offer to a stranger if you only had a brief moment in an elevator together. It pays to be as specific and non-problem-oriented as possible. Now, in truth, complete strangers don't talk to me in the elevator. The elevator speech is really a sentence or two you can offer someone a little closer than a complete stranger—someone who just might be a potential client or referral source.

One approach is to make your elevator speech a simple declarative sentence; for example, "I help therapists transition into successful life coaches." However, this format may inadvertently disqualify a potential client. For example, if the stranger in the elevator with me wasn't a therapist, she might just tune out or think, "Oh well, I guess coaching isn't for me then."

A more open format is more flexible. A more open format can initiate a dialogue rather than just qualify you for a position. So I say, "Well, for example, I help therapists transition into successful life coaches. Are you in any sort of transition?" Now, if the stranger is an accountant thinking about becoming a portrait artist, he has something he can connect with. Here are some examples of how I might respond when someone asks, "What do you mean, a 'life coach'?"

"For example, I work with women who are at transition points in their careers. Have you ever been at a transition point and wanted some support?"

"For example, I focus on helping small business people who are looking for ways to expand their horizons. Have you ever felt like if you could just see things a little differently, things would be better?"

"For example, I support entrepreneurs in the early stages of creating their enterprises. Are there any projects in your life you'd like some support with?"

"For example, I work with top-level managers who are looking for what's next. What's next in your life?"

"For example, I work with people who are very successful in their careers, but are hungry for something else. Ever had that hungry feeling that there must be more to life than this?"

Now it's your turn:

THE ELEVATOR SPEECH WORKSHEET

First, come up with an example of the kind of people you want to coach, then craft a powerful question to ask on the heels of your description.

Scenario: You've been talking to someone at a party for a couple of minutes. She has told you what she does and you've said that you're a life coach. She seems like an interesting person. Then comes the question "What exactly *is* a life coach?"

A one-sentence description of whom you might coach:

_____

_____

Impact follow-up question:

_____

_____

WHAT DO YOU CHARGE FOR YOUR SERVICES?

As therapists, many of us have already had to grapple with this issue. To set our coaching fee we need to first place it in a larger context. How much a year do we want—need—to make as a coach? Remember, to be a successful business owner and entrepreneur, one *must* spend money to make money. If you fail to do so and instead run your business on a shoestring budget, you'll have a shoestring business.

Be open to spending money to begin your coaching business—and be willing to continue to spend money for the sake of your business. This will allow you to grow, both as a coach and as a business.

Things to remember about building your coaching business as you go forward from here:

✓ You *are* the business! Spend money on schooling, training, technology, and whatever else you need to support yourself in building your business and success.

✓   To continue learning throughout your career, you must hire the best coaches you can afford for yourself. (During this transition, it's even better if they themselves were once therapists. Just be sure they're well trained as coaches.)

✓   You must spend money on marketing and promotion. No one can use your services if they don't know that you exist. Over time you will discover which marketing investments pay off in referrals and which are a waste (Hint: forget that ad in the *New York Times*).

✓   You must spend money on business development. Your coaching practice is a business, just like IBM. You are its chief asset. You need to develop your skills in many areas as an entrepreneur. As you do so your business will prosper.

✓   You must cover your own monthly expenses as a business owner. Decide when to take money out of the business and how much to reinvest into the business. Keep reviewing this plan as the market changes. But remember: pay yourself something first.

So, how do you calculate these expenses at the very beginning? Make educated guesses. The first stage in implementing most plans is to have a clear written blueprint, something you can refer to when confusion or circumstances conspire to push you off track.

COACHING SKILL: Write It Out

Goal: To create a document defining your budget.

Tool: Create a written budget plan using the following Marketing Budget Plan Worksheet.

THE MARKETING BUDGET PLAN WORKSHEET

STEP 1: Make a list of the monthly expenses you'll have next year. Items to consider include: rent, office expenses, advertising, travel, conferences, a coach of your own, training, fees, insurance, printing, website design and maintenance, voice mail, other marketing and promotion expenses, an accountant/bookkeeper, postage, quarterly tax payments, capital expenses (big-ticket items that are one-time-only expenses), and money for future expansion and business development. Now, of course, you won't know for certain what these numbers will be. Next year, when you do this again, you'll have much more accurate figures. For the moment just go ahead and guess, estimate, and approximate. This is to be considered a very rough draft.

Monthly Expenses for My Coaching Business

_____

_____

_____

_____

_____

_____

The total monthly cost of my coaching business is: $_____

STEP 2: Now we can begin to create a budget:

Marketing Budget Plan

How much will it cost each month to do all of the things you must do to maintain and grow your business?

    A. _____ (this is the figure from step 1)

How much profit—above the cost of doing business—do you want to make each month from coaching?

    B. _____

Add the previous two lines together to determine how much you need to make each month:

    C. _____

What is your monthly fee per client for coaching? (Just make one up.)

    D. _____

How many clients will you need to make the amount listed in C?

    E. _____

How many hours a week do you want to work providing direct services to coaching clients?

    F. _____

Which variables will you adjust to make this plan work? (For example, you could raise your fee, shorten the length of your sessions, and/or expand the number of your coaching clients.)

_____

_____

_____

_____

_____

_____

Now that you have an idea about what you need to charge, it's time to take a stand on what you actually *are* going to charge. At this point, a whole chorus of inner critics may rise up to sabotage you. One inner critic may want you to give your services away because that's the "good and right" thing to do. It says, "This is such good work in the world. I shouldn't be greedy. I should be generous and give it away!" Another inner critic may not want you to charge much because you aren't worth that much anyway. This critic mutters, "I hardly know what I'm doing so I shouldn't charge anything for such undeveloped coaching." A third inner critic may want to charge some figure it thinks is the right figure and no more, simply because someone else charges that much. "Well, if she charges $200 a month then I couldn't charge more than that."

To leave the inner critic conversation behind you, practice talking about coaching and your services and what it costs to work with you. You'll need to do this many times so that you bleed off the emotional charge surrounding your fees.

COACHING SKILL: Just Do It!

Goal: To make the conversation about what you charge an effortless one.

Tool: Use the following Setting Your Fee Worksheet to become comfortable talking about your fees.

SETTING YOUR FEE WORKSHEET

STEP 1: CHOOSE: Be courageous in asking for your fee. Decide on an amount right now. Stop reading. Close your eyes and do it. Okay, got it? Now add $50.00. This is your fee. Don't hedge! If you hedge on your fee and don't ask for what you want, you may end up feeling resentful or as if you're being taken advantage of once you're actually providing services to your clients.

Your fee: I charge $_____ per month for _____ sessions of _____ minutes length. I also charge $_____ for an initial intake session, which lasts _____ hours.

STEP 2: PRACTICE WHERE IT'S SAFE: Walk over to a mirror and tell yourself your fee. Say the sentence aloud a few times: "I charge $XXX per month for coaching, and $XXX for my initial intake consultation." How does it feel? Does it make you feel sick to your stomach? Does it make you feel powerful? Write about what comes up for you when you speak your fee aloud:

_____

_____

_____

STEP 3: PRACTICE IN THE REAL WORLD: Now go out and practice; tell your fee to twenty people over the next five days. What happened? To you? To them? How did it feel? How did they react? How did you react? What have you created? Write down what you experienced:

_____

_____

_____

_____

_____

_____

_____

_____

_____

_____

_____

_____

_____

WHOM DO YOU TARGET & WHAT DO YOU NEED TO DO TO IMPLEMENT THIS MARKETING PLAN?

The next step in implementing a marketing plan is to identify both who will want to become a client and who will refer clients to you. There are various short-range and long-range strategies for determining appropriate targets for your marketing and promotion campaigns. (If all this talk sounds much too corporate, take a deep breath before continuing.)

From the perspective of HMOs and insurance companies, therapy is an extension of medical treatment; it is a set of treatments designed to ameliorate mental illness. Those who suffer psychological dysfunction seek out professionals who can help them. As a therapist, maintaining an excellent reputation may be the only marketing you need to do.

Coaching is another kettle of fish. It is clearly a luxury item. As such, for private individuals, funding for coaching is in direct competition with entertainment dollars; for corporations, funding is in direct competition with human resource dollars and business consulting and development dollars. Therefore, as coaches, our strategies to acquire clients need to be more aggressive and proactive than we're accustomed to as therapists.

Humans don't like to face their own incompetence at doing unfamiliar activities. Most therapists are unfamiliar with aggressively target-marketing their services. As you learn and practice these new skills, you're probably going to go through an uncomfortable period. Anyone who promises that this will be easy and effortless is deceiving you. But by following the marketing plan you'll have developed by the end of this chapter, you can both succeed as a coach and learn competence in these new skill areas.

Acquiring Clients

The basic process for acquiring new clients is comprised of four simple action steps:

Step 1: Give a potential client a sample session, in which you introduce your approach to coaching and demonstrate how coaching works (see chapter 8 for more information on sample sessions).

Step 2: At the end of this sample session—or in a later call—determine that the client chooses you as his coach.

Step 3: Do an intake session to assess the client's level of satisfaction with all the various areas of her life, identifying the core passions that are important to her, and determining the specific goals and objectives of the coaching the two of you will embark upon (see chapter 7 for more information on intake sessions).

Step 4: Establish up front the coaching schedule, fee payment procedures, and any other practical details of the coaching relationship.

How, though, will you find the potential clients to amaze with sample sessions that sparkle? As mentioned, there are a variety of both short-range and long-range marketing strategies to pursue.

Short-Range Marketing

Your focus in short-range marketing is to get as many coaching clients as possible, as soon as possible. You don't have to go far afield to do this.

As a hotshot coaching marketer your first task is to build a sales force. (This isn't as daunting as it sounds.) The first members of your sales force are everyone who knows you and knows the quality you bring to your work and your relationships. This is known as your *sphere of influence*. Your sphere of influence includes your peers, your neighbors, your family, the people you do business with—in fact, almost anyone you come in contact with except your clients and ex-clients (it's a mistake to create dual relationships with these folks, in my opinion; see chapter 10 for more information on the dangers of a blended practice).

You may wonder, but what do these people know about my coaching? Good question. We've talked about creating sample sessions that sparkle. Here is your chance to try them out.

CREATE YOUR OWN SALES FORCE WORKSHEET

STEP 1: YOUR SPHERE OF INFLUENCE: Make a list of twenty people who know and like you; write their phone number next to their name.

<u>Name</u> <u>Phone Number</u>

1._____

2._____

3._____

4._____

5._____

6._____

7._____

8._____

9._____

10._____

11._____

12._____

13._____

14._____

15._____

16._____

17._____

18._____

19._____

20._____

STEP 2: CALL: Now, call each one of these twenty people and set up a time to do a sample session. Check off a person's name when you've set up a session. At the end of these sample sessions, instead of asking for business, you'll want to say something like, "Now you've had a taste of what coaching is and what I do as a coach. I need your help. What I need is referrals to help build my coaching practice. Do you know a few people I could contact who might be interested in coaching?"

I know this sounds pushy, and you may not be able to do it at first. You'd probably much rather leave it a little vague, like, "So if you know anyone who might like coaching, ask them to give me a call." Try that ending with five referral sources and sit back and wait for the phone to ring—you'll die of old age first.

Even if you're too scared to ask directly for referrals, you *must*, at the very least, give referral sources a packet of your cards and call them the following week to ask if they've thought of anyone who might be interested in coaching. Make the exact same call one month later. If you don't at least do this, you may as well have not done the sample session in the first place. People want to help, but we're all very busy. It's easy to forget. To enroll your sphere of influence into your sales force you have to hound them a little.

Make a commitment, right now, to contact your sphere of influence on a regular basis:

I will contact each person in my sphere of influence and ask for referrals at least _____ times a year.

Signed: _____

Long-Range Marketing

After you've got a few clients you'll want to consider targeting a niche. All marketing begins with identifying who is in need of a particular product or service. Then you whittle this population down. Who can you, as a coach, best serve? What special areas of expertise do you possess? What special hobbies or interests might make you attractive to a potential client? Fill out the Niche Discovery Worksheet that follows and see what draws your interest.

THE NICHE DISCOVERY WORKSHEET

STEP 1: BRAINSTORM ABOUT POTENTIAL SOURCES FOR FUTURE CLIENTS

Write ideas for how to use the following groups of people to help you find clients. Remember, this is brainstorming—don't tell yourself, "That's a stupid idea. It would never work!" Just put it down, the stupider the better. Have fun with this!

Example:

People who share your hobbies:

I love to ride mountain bikes. The guys I ride with keep complaining about not having enough time to ride. I could offer them sample sessions on how to find more time in their lives to ride.

People who share your religious or spiritual practices:

_____

_____

Organizations you participate in:

_____

_____

Groups or organizations you admire:

_____

_____

People who share your hobbies:

_____

_____

People who are passionate about _____:

_____

_____

People who share your political ideas about _____:

_____

_____

People who are involved in _____:

_____

_____

People who, like you, are _____:

_____

_____

People who work in the field of _____:

_____

_____

People who need _____:

_____

_____

Looking at contemporary trends and what's going on in the world, I see I can also find clients from _____:

_____

_____

And from somewhere I never thought of before: _____:

_____

_____

STEP 2: CHOICE

Choose one of these potential niches and list three action steps you can take to design/implement an outreach program for this niche. Pick the niche that has the most passion, interest, and juice for you.

Example:

Niche: *People who share my hobbies.*

Action step 1: *Write article for mountain biking newsletter.*

Action step 2: *Offer Fred a sample session.*

Action step 3: *Organize a day that's a ride, potluck, and workshop on life balance.*

Niche:

_____

Action step 1:

_____

Planned date of implementation: _____ Actual date of implementation: _____

Date of completion: _____

Action step 2:

_____

Planned date of implementation: _____ Actual date of implementation: _____

Date of completion: _____

Action step 3:

_____

Planned date of implementation: _____ Actual date of implementation: _____

Date of completion: _____

HOW DO YOU DIFFERENTIATE YOURSELF FROM OTHER COACHES?

As a therapist, it's perfectly acceptable to be a little self-effacing. After all, you're there to serve clients' needs, not your own narcissistic desires. The kind of coaching that this book advocates comes from this same tradition, placing the wisdom and creativity of the client above your own opinions and insights. However, when it comes to marketing, it's time to take your light out from underneath that bushel and let it shine.

This can be a bit uncomfortable for us as therapists who typically let reputation, connections, and track record do the marketing for us. However, since coaching is a luxury item—not a necessity—your services as a coach are in direct competition with everything from a new car to a cruise to the Bahamas.

If you try to sell how great coaching itself is, you'll help the rest of the coaching profession, but you may not fill up your practice. Instead, you need to sell yourself as the best coach a potential client could have. To do this, you have to separate yourself from the pack of coaches out there already providing coaching services. You have to be the red fish in a school of yellow fish.

Since you don't have years of experience as a coach yet, this can seem a bit daunting at first. But remember, coaching isn't consulting. You don't need a huge experience base to coach. All you need is a deep faith in the resourcefulness and creativity of your client.

What can you do to set yourself apart? Pull out your trumpet, get ready to blow your horn, and fill out the following Assets Worksheet.

ASSETS WORKSHEET

What skills, talents, hobbies, interests, life experiences, and other qualities do you possess that make you unique—and which can you capitalize on in marketing your coaching practice?

Skills:

_____

_____

_____

_____

_____

Special talents:

_____

_____

_____

Hobbies and interests:

_____

_____

_____

Interesting and different life experiences:

_____

_____

_____

Other unusual qualities about yourself:

_____

_____

_____

_____

(continues on next page)

Now, reread this list and ask yourself how you can utilize three of these assets to target niche markets.

Example:

Asset: *I write mysteries.*

Possible niche markets: *Other writers.*

Action step: *Conduct workshop at a writers' conference on a coaching topic.*

Asset 1:

_____

Possible niche markets:_____

_____

Asset 2:

_____

Possible niche markets: _____

_____

Asset 3:

_____

Possible niche markets:_____

_____

Choose one of these markets and design an action plan to capitalize on this personal asset and acquire clients.

Action step:

_____

_____

_____

Planned date of implementation: _____ Actual date of implementation: _____

Date of completion: _____

The following is a more general Assets Worksheet you can use with your clients:

ASSETS WORKSHEET

This worksheet will help you identify the personal qualities you have—both already known qualities and unexpected qualities—that you can capitalize on to advance projects in your life.

Skills:

_____
_____
_____
_____
_____

Special talents:

_____
_____
_____

Hobbies and interests:

_____
_____
_____
_____

Interesting and different life experiences:

_____
_____
_____
_____

Other unusual qualities about yourself:

_____
_____
_____
_____

YOUR MARKETING PLAN

Let's complete your personally tailored marketing plan. We now have some beginning answers to our initial questions:

How do you describe your services?

What do you charge?

Whom do you target?

What do you need to do to implement this marketing plan?

How do you differentiate yourself from other coaches?

Go ahead and fill out your marketing plan:

MY MARKETING PLAN

From the Elevator Speech Worksheet:

My short description of my services is:

_____

_____

_____

From the Marketing Budget Plan Worksheet:

I work _____ hours a month, I have _____ clients, and I make _____ a year from coaching.

From the Setting Your Fee Worksheet:

I charge _____ a month for _____ sessions each of which are _____ in length.

From the Create Your Own Sales Force Worksheet:

I will contact each person in my sphere of influence and ask for referrals at least _____ times a year.

From the Niche Discovery Worksheet and the Assets Worksheet:

I am targeting two niches and have identified the first action steps I need to take for each niche:

Niche 1: _____

Action step: _____

_____

Planned date of implementation: _____ Actual date of implementation: _____

Date of completion: _____

Niche 2: _____

Action step: _____

_____

Planned date of implementation: _____ Actual date of implementation: _____

Date of completion: _____

Congratulations! Now it's time to get inspired by Nike commercials and *just do it*! The next chapter will help you do exactly that.

CHAPTER TWELVE

ONGOING MARKETING & PROMOTION

For entrepreneurs in the service profession, every day is a job interview. My father, who once made a living selling freezers door-to-door, put it this way: "Selling yourself is like pouring actions into a big funnel. You just keep pouring things in the top: advertising, knocking on doors, cold-calling. You never know exactly what works, so you do it all. Eventually, if you persevere, customers start coming out of the bottom of the funnel. Some of them come from what you did. Some of them just seem to show up magically. But you've got to keep pouring your actions into the top of that funnel for magic to occur."

It isn't enough to implement a couple of action steps and then sit back and wait for clients to pour in. Selling your coaching services needs to be a regular part of your life, not a one-time project.

This may sound a bit like a grind. That's why a group of coaches, myself included, designed a tool called *Success Coach 100* (Dickerson, Skibbins, & Skibbins, 2004). Success Coach 100 makes marketing and self-promotion more like a game, less like an onerous task. The tool's other creators have given me permission to share it with you, in hopes that you, too, will come to enjoy marketing.

SUCCESS COACH 100

Welcome to Success Coach 100! With this simple but powerful self-accountability tool, you will be able to:

✓ Track the actions you take that lead to marketing success.

✓ Assess how well you are implementing your marketing plan.

✓ Generate new ideas for marketing, and implement them.

✓ Celebrate your successes as you build your practice.

Directions

Here are the step-by-step instructions for using Success Coach 100:

OVERVIEW OF THE FORM/CHART

The numbers along the longer edge of the page represent the days of the month, days one to thirty-one. The numbers along the shorter edge represent the number of points you have earned for each completed action that builds your full practice. Shade in each box for every 2 points that you earn.

The goal of each day that you do marketing work is to earn 100 points. Full-time coaches need to devote at least two days a week to marketing their coaching business. That means at least two 100-point days a week.

Let's see how you do that …

HOW TO EARN POINTS

You earn a specific number of points for each action that you take to build your business. Here are some examples:

✓ Get a client. You just earned 100 points!

✓ Give a one-hour teleclass during which you ask for referrals and/or sample sessions. Yeah! You just earned 50 points!

✓ Set up a sample session. Log 26 points into your chart!

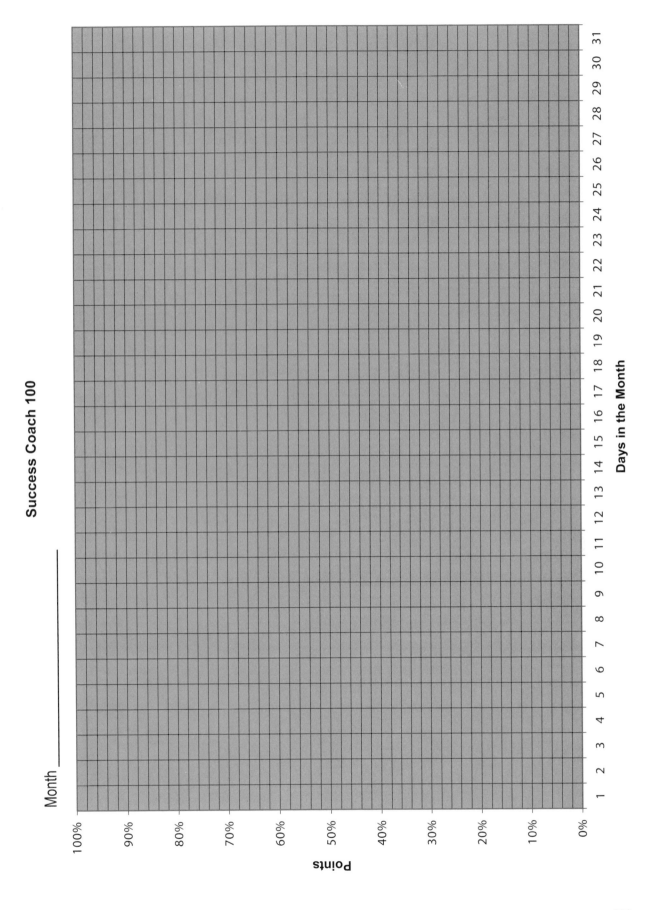

✓   Initiate a conversation in which you talk about coaching. Wow! You just earned 10 points: shade in 5 boxes!

✓   Leave a message or a voice mail where you talk about coaching. That's worth 2 points per message—pretty cool!

      (See the following list, Success Actions, for a complete table of points.)

Keep a running total of your points. The minute you achieve 100 points you can stop marketing for the day! Walk out of your office and give yourself a small but special nurturing treat or experience.

In any given week in which you earn 500 points, give yourself a day of luxury! In any month in which you earn 2,000 points, take a week off from marketing your coaching business and find an exceptional way to celebrate your success. Hawaii anyone?

The following is an example of the tool in action:

A DAY IN THE LIFE OF "MARGE, THE CERTIFIED COACH"

Marge woke up early, drank her morning coffee, and walked into her home office, ready to build her coaching career. She opened her contact management system and chose ten names from her sphere of influence to call.

She made all ten calls. One number was disconnected. She left six messages on voice mail. In each of these voice mail messages she talked about coaching and asked the person to call her back to set up a free sample session. She earned 18 points and shaded in 9 boxes on the Success Coach 100 form.

She spoke to three people. She was politely rebuffed by one person. With the other two, she had conversations about coaching. One of them asked her to call back in two months. The other scheduled a sample session with her. After making these calls she sent thank-you cards to the two people she talked with who were interested in coaching. She earned 10 points per call for the people that she talked to, totaling 30 points. She earned 26 more points for scheduling a sample session. She also earned 6 additional points per thank-you card.

She made one call to a past client and asked for a referral. The woman promised to call her back the next day with a lead. Marge started to shade in an additional 13 boxes. Then she realized that she had earned over 100 points. She said, "Yee-haw!" Her marketing was done for the day. She called a friend and spent the afternoon at her favorite local golf course.

Success Actions: Table of Points

The following is a list of success actions that MyFullPractice.com recommends you take, with point values that correspond to each. Make sure to mark on your form each point that you earn, every day!

FACE-TO-FACE OR VOICE-TO-EAR:

✓ Get a client. This includes setting up the intake/first session and receiving payment for the intake/first session in advance.

100 points

✓ Give a sample session in which you ask the person to be your client or give you referrals.

76 points

✓ Walk up to someone you don't know, strike up a conversation about coaching, and ask her or him for a sample session.

76 points

✓ Fire your least favorite client from your practice.

30 points

✓ Set up a sample session with an actual date entered in your calendar.

26 points

✓ Call an existing coaching client or past coaching client and ask for referrals.

26 points

✓ Refer a coaching client—or potential coaching client—that you don't want to work with to another coach.

10 points

✓ Call and offer a person in your sphere of influence a sample of your coaching.

10 points

✓ Have a conversation (in person or on the phone) where you talk about coaching. In that conversation ask at least one of these things: "Will you do a sample session with me?" "Will you give me referrals?" or "Will you be my client?" We don't suggest that you ask all of these things in each conversation … but it couldn't hurt!

10 points

✓ Set up a sample coaching session with a successful coach who can refer you business.

10 points

✓ Complete a sample coaching session with a successful coach and ask for referrals.

26 points

✓ Set up a time and date to meet with a person who could potentially give you referrals.

10 points

✓ Meet with a person who could send you referrals and ask for those referrals.

10 points

✓ Call a coaching client just to tell them you're thinking of them.

10 points

✓ Ask a client for feedback on your coaching and how it could be better.

6 points per client

✓ Leave a message or a voice mail where you talk about coaching; in this message, ask at least one of these three things: "Will you do a sample session with me?" "Will you give me referrals?" or "Will you be my client?"

2 points

IN A CROWD:

✓ Give a teleclass to your clients and prospects where you ask for referrals and/or sample sessions. Let your topic be one about which you have passion or expertise!

One-hour teleclass: 50 points

✓ Go to a networking meeting where you talk to at least *five* people about being a coach; give out your business card and collect cards from these same individuals.

26 points

✓ Follow up with all those people whose cards you collected from the networking meeting via telephone and tell them how much you enjoyed meeting them!

5 points per person

✓ Do a workshop or speak to a group of people where, as part of your talk/workshop, you ask for referrals or sample sessions.

26 points

✓ Go to a meeting where your ideal clients tend to congregate.

20 points

FOR YOURSELF:

✓ Go to an all-day training program to enhance your coaching, business, or life skills.

100 points per day

✓ Hire a personal assistant to do business and personal work for you.

100 points

✓ Create a contact management system where you can track all of your prospects and referral sources.

100 points

✓ Sign up and pay for an ongoing group that provides an accountable environment focused on building your practice.

100 points

✓ Hire a coach and send a check to do the intake session or first month of coaching.

100 points

✓ Get an hour of supervision on the coaching that *you* do with *your* clients.

76 points

✓ Have a session with *your* coach (a session that you pay for).

50 points

✓ Take an hour-long teleclass in which you actively participate on the call. This class must be designed to enhance your coaching, business, or life skills.

10 points

✓ Write a paragraph describing your ideal client.

10 points

✓ Read aloud your ideal client paragraph.

2 points

WITH A STAMP:

✓ Send a card to someone in your sphere of influence for no reason at all.

6 points

✓ Write and send a thank-you card to a coaching prospect or a referral source.

6 points

✓ Send a thank-you card to someone who gave you a referral.

6 points

✓ Send a handwritten birthday card to a coaching client, prospect, or someone who is in your sphere of influence.

10 points

✓ Send a thank-you card to an existing client.

10 points

✓ Send out a newsletter to coaching clients, prospects, and your sphere of influence. This can be in e-mail format or by postal mail.

26 points

ON THE COMPUTER:

✓ Compile a list of names, addresses, phone numbers, and e-mail addresses of all the people you know (past business associates, past club associations, Christmas card lists, neighbors, virtual communities, temple or church contacts, family, friends, all the people you have talked to about coaching or have ever done a sample session with, past coaching clients, and current coaching clients. Think of who else you want on that list). This is your list of people in your sphere of influence.

50 points

✓ Enter your sphere of influence list into your contact management system.

2 points per contact

✓ Enter a *new* contact you have made into your existing contact management system.

4 points

✓ Design and/or work on your newsletter or e-zine.

6 points per hour

✓ Send out a newsletter to coaching clients, prospects, and your sphere of influence. This can be in e-mail format or by postal mail.

26 points

✓ Contact one of your current coaching clients (not during their coaching time with you) and offer them a free session of coaching for every person they refer to you who ends up scheduling a sample session of coaching.

10 points

✓ Contact one of your current coaching clients and, in a personal way, offer them a month of free coaching for every person that they refer who becomes a paying client.

10 points

✓ Work on your Web site—write content, look at graphics, talk to your Web designer, and edit what you have already created.

6 points per hour

✓ Send your ideal client paragraph to your sphere of influence and ask for referrals of anyone who fits this description.

4 points per person

✓ Send an e-mail to your sphere of influence that describes your coaching services. The e-mail must include a request for a sample session and/or referrals.

2 points

Use the Success Coach 100 to set yourself attainable marketing goals—even if they're as humble as "I'll earn 100 points by Friday." If you do so, you'll find that clients begin showing up. Do nothing—or do a little in a spurt and then sit back and wait—and soon you'll decide that you can't succeed in this business. And that would be sad. Because the problem wouldn't be that you *couldn't* succeed, it would be that you didn't fully implement a plan to succeed. You can do this!

Success Coach 100

Month _____

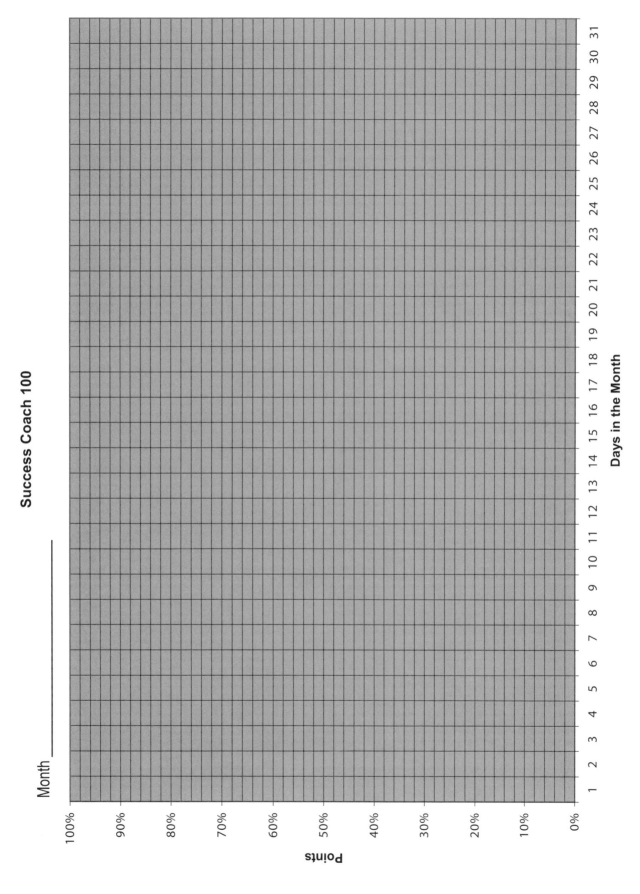

Points

Days in the Month

CHAPTER THIRTEEN

KEEP YOUR EYES ON THE PRIZE!

There is a well-known saying: "When you're up to your hips in alligators it's hard to remember that you set out that morning to drain the swamp." On the path to establishing a successful coaching practice, alligators abound. Some may take the form of biting comments from your family, "All that education, and you're just a coach now?" or your peers, "Coaching—isn't that like cheerleading or something?" But the biggest alligators of all are self-generated: "This is too hard!" or "What business do you have coaching someone like that?" or "You're above this kind of work!" or "I feel like a used-car salesman."

Alligator wrestling is a great skill to have on board. But let's also look at the bigger vision: the plan to drain the swamp—or in your case, the intention to become a successful coach. In the service of keeping true to this plan, complete the following exercise:

THE BIG PICTURE

It's five years in the future, and you have a coaching practice that exceeds all of your expectations. Describe your life by answering the following questions:

1. Where do you live and how has that changed in the past five years?

2. What adventures have you undertaken because coaching gave you the additional financial security you desired?

3. What do you like best about your coaching work?

4. What parts of your administrative, marketing, and promotion work have you been able to turn over to your staff, in order to free up your own time?

5. If you could give an image or a gift to that earlier you who is reading this book to inspire that you to persevere through the rough spots ahead, what would it be?

Now, accept this gift from your future successful self; find a way to use this exercise to remind yourself of the big picture. (When I did this exercise I received a Rolex. I kept a picture of that watch right by my phone to inspire me. I now own the watch.)

Remember: if you want something deeply enough, you can attain it. You may need a dream, a plan, action steps, support, a little luck, and a lot of persistence, but it will come to you.

I'll end with two quotes I've placed by my computer screen to inspire me, in hopes that they will do the same for you:

> *Nothing in the world can take the place of persistence.*
> *Talent will not; nothing is more common than unsuccessful*
> *men with talent. Genius will not; unrewarded genius*
> *is almost a proverb. Education will not; the world is full of*
> *educated derelicts. Persistence and determination alone are*
> *omnipotent. The slogan "Press on" has solved and always*
> *will solve the problems of the human race.*
> —Calvin Coolidge

> *Whatever you can do or dream you can, begin it.*
> *Boldness has genius, power, and magic in it.*
> —Johann Wolfgang von Goethe

Best of luck, coach.

REFERENCES

Alcoholics Anonymous World Services, Inc. (2002). *The Big Book of Alcoholics Anonymous*. New York: Alcoholics Anonymous World Services Incorporated.

Carson, R., & Rogers, N. (1990). *Taming your gremlin*. New York: HarperCollins.

Dickerson, M., Skibbins, M., & Skibbins, D. (2004). *Success Coach 100*. Retrieved December 12, 2004, from www.MyFullPractice.com

Gallwey, T. (1997). *The inner game of tennis*. New York: Random House.

Grodzki, L., & Allen, W. (2005). *The business and practice of coaching*. New York: W. W. Norton and Company.

Whitmore, J. (2002). *Coaching for performance*. London: Nicholas Brealey Publishing.

Whitworth, L., Kimsey-House, H. & Sandahl, P. (1998). *Co-active coaching: New skills for coaching people toward success in work and life*. Mountain View, CA: Davies-Black Publishing.

Whorf, B. (1964). *Language, thought, and reality: selected writings*. Cambridge, MA: MIT Press.

David Skibbins, Ph.D., CPCC, is a licensed psychotherapist and practicing life coach. He lives on the Northern California coast with his brilliant wife and his frisky Portuguese Water Dog. David Skibbins' first mystery, *Eight of Swords*, won the St. Martin's Best Traditional Mystery Contest. www.davidskibbins.com

Foreword writer Mary E. Olk, Ph.D., CPCC, is a certified professional co-active coach with the Coaches Training Institute.

REFERENCES

Alcoholics Anonymous World Services, Inc. (2002). *The Big Book of Alcoholics Anonymous.* New York: Alcoholics Anonymous World Services Incorporated.

Carson, R., & Rogers, N. (1990). *Taming your gremlin.* New York: HarperCollins.

Dickerson, M., Skibbins, M., & Skibbins, D. (2004). *Success Coach 100.* Retrieved December 12, 2004, from www.MyFullPractice.com

Gallwey, T. (1997). *The inner game of tennis.* New York: Random House.

Grodzki, L., & Allen, W. (2005). *The business and practice of coaching.* New York: W. W. Norton and Company.

Whitmore, J. (2002). *Coaching for performance.* London: Nicholas Brealey Publishing.

Whitworth, L., Kimsey-House, H. & Sandahl, P. (1998). *Co-active coaching: New skills for coaching people toward success in work and life.* Mountain View, CA: Davies-Black Publishing.

Whorf, B. (1964). *Language, thought, and reality: selected writings.* Cambridge, MA: MIT Press.

David Skibbins, Ph.D., CPCC, is a licensed psychotherapist and practicing life coach. He lives on the Northern California coast with his brilliant wife and his frisky Portuguese Water Dog. David Skibbins' first mystery, *Eight of Swords*, won the St. Martin's Best Traditional Mystery Contest. www.davidskibbins.com

Foreword writer Mary E. Olk, Ph.D., CPCC, is a certified professional co-active coach with the Coaches Training Institute.